The Armistice and the Aftermath

The Armistice and the Aftermath

The Story in Art

John Fairley

Pen & Sword
MILITARY

First published in Great Britain in 2018 by
Pen & Sword Military
an imprint of
Pen & Sword Books Ltd
47 Church Street
Barnsley
South Yorkshire
S70 2AS

ISBN 978 1 52672 118 1

A CIP catalogue record for this book is available from the British Library

Typeset in Ehrhardt by
Mac Style
Printed and bound in India by Replika Press Pvt. Ltd.

Pen & Sword Books Limited incorporates the imprints of Atlas, Archaeology, Aviation, Discovery, Family History, Fiction, History, Maritime, Military, Military Classics, Politics, Select, Transport, True Crime, Air World, Frontline Publishing, Leo Cooper, Remember When, Seaforth Publishing, The Praetorian Press, Wharncliffe Local History, Wharncliffe Transport, Wharncliffe True Crime and White Owl.

For a complete list of Pen & Sword titles please contact
PEN & SWORD BOOKS LIMITED
47 Church Street, Barnsley, South Yorkshire, S70 2AS, England
E-mail: enquiries@pen-and-sword.co.uk
Website: www.pen-and-sword.co.uk

Contents

Armistice, 1918, Pierre Bonnard.

Chapter One

Peace at Last

Pierre Bonnard's painting of Armistice night in Paris in 1918 is the most joyous picture of the most joyous day in the twentieth century. All the colour and verve of this most passionate of Impressionist artists is devoted to a scene of happiness and relief, yet it also seems to evoke the memory of the killings and carnage which had only ceased that very morning. The beautiful girl at the centre of the painting, entranced, it would seem, by the celebrations around her, perhaps also reflects a consciousness of the dreadful events of the last four years.

But for the men in the foreground, indeed the whole of the rest of the exuberant crowd, there are, it seems, no such inhibitions. The dancers and the diners are flinging themselves into the pleasures of peace. There are watchers at every window. The total blackness recedes and the bright blues and reds assert the confidence of that unique night.

It is in the poems and the paintings that the First World War stays in the minds and imagination of present generations. The painters were there at the heart of great events. So too were the poets, putting into words what the painters depicted on canvas. And both of them trying to illuminate what was happening in the aftermath of war.

Wilfred Owen was to die only seven days before the Armistice while his regiment was crossing the Sambre Oise canal as part of the assaults which were to finally convince Ludendorff and the German generals that they had to sue for peace. He left behind a poem that has continued to arouse emotions a hundred years on:

> Move him into the sun
> Gently its touch awoke him once
> At home, whispering of fields unsown
> Always it woke him even in France
> Until this morning, and this snow
> If anything might rouse him now
> The kind old sun will know.
>
> Think how it wakes the seeds
> Woke, once, the clays of a cold star
> Are limbs so dear achieved, are sides
> Full nerved – still warmed – too hard to stir?
> Was it for this the clay grew tall?
> O what made fatuous sunbeams toil
> To break earth's sleep at all?

Wilfred Owen, like his friend and inspiration Siegfried Sassoon, had been wounded and yet gone back to war.

When the guns fell silent, Siegfried Sassoon wrote what was to become the Anthem of the Armistice.

> Everyone suddenly burst out singing
> And I was filled with such delight
> As prisoned birds must find in freedom
> Winging wildly across the white
> Orchards and dark green fields, on, on, and out of sight.
>
> Everyone's voice was suddenly lifted
> And beauty came like the setting sun
> My heart was shaken with tears; and horror
> Drifted away. O, but everyone
> Was a bird and the song was wordless; the singing will never be done.

Sassoon, wounded once more in July 1918 and shipped back to England, had felt an intense longing to be back at the Front with his company – 'There at least I had been something real, and I had lived myself into a feeling of responsibility for them. All that was decent in me disliked leaving them to endure what I had escaped.'

In the first days of November, Sassoon had found himself recovered enough to rejoin the literary world, of which he was already a star. He met Winston Churchill, 'Full of victory talk, and just off to a War Cabinet meeting'. The next day, he took a train down to the West Country to stay with Thomas Hardy, who told him that 'in 1914 he feared more than anything else that English literature might be wiped out by the Germans.' Then it was back to Oxford to meet John Masefield. Sassoon's diary for November 11 reads:

I was walking in the water meadows by the river below Cuddesdon – a quiet grey day. A jolly peal of bells was ringing from the village church, and the villagers were hanging little flags out of the windows of their thatched houses. The war is ended. It is impossible to realise. Oxford had much flag waving also.

I got to London about 6.30 and found masses of people in streets and congested Tubes, all waving flags and making fools of themselves – an outburst of mob patriotism. It was a wretched wet night and very mild. It is a loathsome ending to the loathsome tragedy of the last four years.

Robert Graves, recovered from wounds sustained at the Battle of the Somme, was at a camp in Wales when the Armistice came – 'The news sent me out walking along the dyke above the marshes of Rhuddlan, cursing and sobbing and thinking of the dead.'

The artists and poets coming back from the war brought its horrors with them in their minds. As Graves wrote, 'Shells used to come bursting on my bed at midnight. Strangers, in daytime, would assume the faces of friends who had been killed.'

One of the most notable official war artists, Christopher Richard Nevinson, a wounded veteran who had painted La Mitrailleuse and Passchendaele, was in London that day when the news came through. He wrote:

> For me, Armistice Day will always remain the most remarkable day of emotion in my life. When we heard the cheers outside, I dropped my brushes and rushed out with Kathleen. We jumped on a lorry which took us down to Whitehall. Here we saw Winston Churchill beaming on a mob that was yelling itself hoarse. With a thousand others in Trafalgar Square we danced Knees Up Mother Brown, then to the Café Royal for food, where we were joined by a gang of officers and drank a good deal of champagne, and raided the kitchens because the staff had knocked off work. Then on to the Studio Club to find a crowd of demi-intellectuals terribly calm and indifferent to the noise of the multitude, and some of them even apprehensive as they saw the end of their well-paid jobs. Back into the streets to rejoice with human beings. And back again to the Café Royal: poor Kathleen with an American cocotte lying over her knees crying, and another girl sobbing because no one was cheering for Serbia – though she came from Birmingham. A crowd of journalists, including Scott of the Manchester Guardian, who, for no reason at all, was bitten by a French girl, who then bit me.

Nevinson and Scott went searching for a pharmacy in Piccadilly to treat their wounds. Then it was back to the Café Royal.

> We were joined by Generals, subalterns, and grave literary men who wished to discuss the peace terms with Scott. I could not bear to listen, and, with some others, I climbed the pillars of the old cafe instead. Often I marvel how this was done!

Armistice Day in 1918 was, indeed, probably the most passionately celebrated day in the whole of the twentieth century. As the guns fell silent, vast crowds poured on to the streets of towns and cities all across the Western world. And everywhere the foremost artists of the day were impelled to try and convey the emotions of those moments.

Gilbert Beal recorded the night that the news reached New York, and George Luks the reaction in Philadelphia. The Irish painter William Orpen was in Amiens.

But then the tense and difficult process of trying to make the peace ensued. Orpen and the English painter Augustus John were to be appointed official artists at the Versailles conference, through the months of discussion and debate and then the ceremonial signing of the final agreement; Orpen's pictures of the signing were to be described by the Royal Academician Sir John Lavery as masterpieces.

The artists had had unique access to the extraordinary closing events of the war, including the surrender of the entire German battle fleet out in the North Sea. Their paintings are an intense and revealing record of the momentous days which led up to the ceasefire, and then of the redrawing of the maps of Europe, the Middle East and Africa.

Armistice Day, Paris. Frank Myers Boggs.

Chapter Two

Paris

On the afternoon of Armistice Day, the French Prime Minister Georges Clemenceau made his announcement to the French parliament that the guns had fallen silent. The war was over. Then he went home, where his great friend Claude Monet was waiting.

The artists who had been commissioned as official painters, or those who had been drawn inevitably to record such momentous times, had found themselves living and working at the heart of the events which led up to and followed the Armistice.

They were following closely as the Allied armies rolled back the German troops. They saw the broken towns and villages where the fighting had been fiercest. At the same time some of them were portraying the untouched life of the countryside where the guns could be heard, but the shells never fell.

Later, as the peace conference opened at Versailles and the statesmen of the victorious Allies, from President Woodrow Wilson to Sheikh Feisal, met to shape the new world order, the painters, Augustus John, William Orpen and others, were given prime positions to observe and record it all. Their work was to give a vivid picture of those times when it seemed the war to end wars had achieved its purpose; and how varied were the hopes and fears of the men who had fought and survived.

On Armistice night Monet and Clemenceau ate supper together. The former had known the latter through much of his turbulent political career. Through the war, Clemenceau had been fiercely critical of what he saw as the inadequacies of the French government's response, and from 1917 onwards had entertained the dark suspicion that some French politicians wanted, in effect, to surrender to the Germans.

When he came to power at the start of 1918, almost his first act was to accuse and then imprison the former Prime Minister Cailleaux, for treasonable discussions with the Germans. Then he fired the French commander Sarrail and, after discussions with the Allies, installed Marshal Foch as supreme commander of the Allied forces.

With the Germans close enough to be shelling and bombing Paris, Clemenceau's activist policies gained him great support, as did his frequent visits to the troops in the trenches – often within sight and range of German positions. His speech to the French Parliament that afternoon of Armistice Day produced ecstatic applause

Right up to that moment on 11 November – though the tide of war had plainly been turning – Paris had remained the sombre city recorded by the painter John Lavery. There had been remonstrations against his wife for not wearing black like all the other women. 'Dirty streets, shutters up,' he wrote. 'Mostly old men and women. Everyone looked sad.' He went to his old haunts in the Latin Quarter, where 'it was as if a deadly plague had swept the place.'

The eleventh hour of the eleventh day transformed all that …

That night, the American Frank Myers Boggs, too, took his paints straight out into the city and recorded the gathering multitude. Boggs came from Ohio, but he had learned his skills in Paris and eventually became a naturalized Frenchman. He painted the Place de la Concorde with its flag-bedecked arch and colourful women and children in the foreground of a busy scene, the like of which Paris had not enjoyed for many a day.

Chapter Three

Forebodings

The array of paintings of Armistice Day and Night across the Western world on that 11 November 1918 are perhaps the most exuberant, colourful, and triumphant works in the whole of that dramatic century. Bonnard, in fact, painted five large canvases of the scenes which unfolded before his eyes in Paris that day.

But as the crowds celebrated victory, the sentiments of many of the participants in the war were laden with foreboding, apprehension and regret, as well as triumph. The American commander in Europe was bitterly opposed to halting the Allied advances. 'This will just be a twenty-year ceasefire,' he was to pronounce, with dreadfully accurate foresight.

Harry S. Truman, destined a quarter of a century later to be called upon to make the single most lethal decision in history, was an American Army artillery officer determined to pulverize the Germans to the last minute of the last hour.

Lady Cynthia Asquith recorded in her diary:

I am beginning to rub my eyes at the prospect of peace. I think it will require more courage than anything that has gone before. It isn't until one leaves off spinning round that one realises how giddy one is. One will have to look at long vistas again, instead of short ones, and one will at last fully recognise that the dead are not only dead for the duration of the war.

The soldiers on the newly silent battlefronts dreamed of Roman triumphal marches through the enemy's cities. John Glubb, later to be renowned in the Middle East as Glubb Pasha, was then a twenty-one-year-old Royal Engineer. His troops were involved in a serious push only three days before the Armistice. He was watching his men feeding their horses when, as he wrote in his diary, 'A mounted orderly rode up and told us that the war was over. A dreadful blow! I was just beginning to enjoy it and this will finish my dreams of the dashing column of pursuit.' Instead, he straightaway ordered his troops to polish their boots, unpack their best uniforms, and prepare to roll forward into a conquered land. But it was not be.

The victories of the Allied armies, pushing inexorably towards the Rhine in October and November, made many of the troops eager to fight on till the Germans surrendered.

Throughout these last weeks of the war, the British, the Canadians, the Australians and the Americans were accompanied by some of the finest artists of the day, commissioned as official painters. They witnessed and portrayed the desperate and implacable fighting as the Allies finally broke through and pushed the German armies back. Some of the unique moments of the Armistice could only be portrayed by the artists out at sea, in the desert, in the air.

The very next day after his dinner with Clemenceau, Monet told the President he wished to present his Water Lilies paintings to the French people. 'They could be a space of tranquillity, a refuge from their wounds, somewhere they could heal their souls with the spectacle of nature and eternity,' he said.

These vast paintings, now curving round their modern gallery in Paris, remain to this day that spectacle which Monet hoped to bestow on his fellow citizens.

Water Lilies, Claude Monet.

Chapter Four

Marshal Foch

William Orpen, the Irish painter, had been one of the first official war artists and closely followed what turned out in 1918 to be the last months of desperate fighting as first the Germans launched what they intended to be the conclusive drive to the Channel coast, and then the Allies' responded with their own offensive.

It is only possible to gaze on William Orpen's portrait of Marshal Foch with awed wonderment. The Marshal with his majestic moustache relaxes, hand in pocket, leaning against a stairway in a pose which he contentedly adopted for an hour and a half every morning for five consecutive days, until the artist was satisfied.

Yet this is August 1918. Foch was Commander-in-Chief of all the Allied armies. He had just launched the great series of attacks which were to finish the war. Though he could not have known it, his opponent Ludendorff had already named the opening assault on 8 August 'the black day of the German army'.

Orpen had wandered down to Foch's headquarters at Bon Bon early in the month to see if the Marshal would permit a portrait. General Weygand took him in to see Foch, and Orpen recalled:

There was the great little man, deep in the study of his maps, very calm, very quiet. He would certainly sit. How long did I want him for? An hour and a half each day, for four or five days? Certainly. When did I wish to start? The next day? Certainly.

I got up very early the next morning and arrived about 6.15 a m. Nobody seemed to be about, and as the only way I knew to get to the library was through the map room, I opened the door. There he was, deep in study. He got up, shook hands and said he would be with me at 7 a m.

During all the time he was sitting, great battles were going on. News was brought to him about every ten minutes. If it was good he would say, 'Bon'. If it was bad he just made a strange noise by forcing air out through his lips.

It seemed amazing, the calmness of that chateau at Bon Bon. Yet wires from that old country house were conveying messages of blood and hell to millions of men. What must the little man have felt? The responsibility of it all, hidden in the brain behind those kind, thoughtful eyes. Apparently his only worry was 'ma pipe'.

Foch had been introduced by the English to pipe-smoking. But it fell to Orpen to bring in feathers and cotton wool and teach him how to clean it. Writing after the war, Orpen revealed an episode that might well have ended in his introduction to the firing squad:

> Foch obviously thought I knew no French. One morning a General came in and the Marshal, very quietly, gave him times, dates, places where battles would be fought up to the end of December 1918, naming the French, British, American divisions which would be used in each. When I got back to my room, I wrote down some dates and places I remembered, and as far as I could judge, everything went exactly as he said it would till about the middle of October. Then the Boche really got on the run. Things went quicker than expected.

Foch had been appointed overall Commander-in-Chief in April 1918, after the alarming success of the German spring offensive. He was both a soldier and an academic strategist, and believed with missionary zeal in the power of attack and surprise. Through the spring and summer of 1918 the Germans were halted and then the Allied offensives planned.

As Foch was posing in the library, his armies were launching nearly 500 tanks towards the old Somme battlefield and taking more than 20,000 prisoners. Every few days there were new offensives towards the Hindenburg line.

Ludendorff, by contrast, was losing his nerve. In his Supreme Command headquarters in Belgium he started raging at the Kaiser's lack of support, at the waste of resources on the Navy and its submarines, and at the defeatist Reichstag. Finally, he fell in a fit on the floor. On his recovery he told the German government that they had to seek an armistice.

At the beginning of October the German government wrote to United States President Wilson, on the back of the Fourteen Points he had previously laid out, seeking an armistice. Wilson, however, replied in the toughest terms, effectively demanding surrender.

Foch, meanwhile, as Orpen had heard, was pushing through his series of attacks. And on the Eastern Front, all the advantage that Germany had gained by doing a deal with the Russian Bolsheviks was being eroded, first by the sudden collapse of their Bulgarian allies in September, then the submission of the Turks in October, and finally the collapse of the Austrians.

As November came, mutinies mushroomed in the German fleet and revolutionary groups arose in every German city. Finally, with the Kaiser fleeing to neutral Holland and the socialist Ebert appointed prime minister, German emissaries were sent to the forest of Compiègne.

Foch awaited them.

Opposite: *Marshal Foch*, Sir William Orpen.

Chapter Five

The Final Battles

Orpen, who had gone home ill after his sessions with Foch, returned to France in October 1918. His paintings of those final few weeks, as the Allies advanced, have a bleakness which gives no hint of impending peace:

> I went out to see the damage done to Bailleul. In a few days British artillery had flattened it out as badly as Ypres. One could hardly find out where the main square had been. Now one could wander all over the Ypres Salient. Was there ever a more ghastly place? Even the Somme was outdone. Mud, water, battered tanks, hundreds of them, battered pillboxes, everything battered and torn, with Ypres like a skeleton.
>
> I went to see Locre – a ghastly place – the fighting must have been terrific. Shell holes full of dead Germans. Everything smashed to pulp. I should imagine, before Hell visited it, Locre must have been a very pretty little place.

This was the setting for The End of a Hero and A Tank, for the (battered indeed) General Birdwood Returning to his Headquarters, for A Skeleton in a Trench, for the skull-laden picture Thiepval, and for Dead German in a Trench.

Orpen travelled with some of the staff, close behind the advancing troops. He wondered at the great fortified German tunnel in the Canal du Nord – 'What a stronghold! It seemed impossible that the Boche could have been driven out of it.' But all along he was overwhelmed by sympathy and admiration for the British soldier. His cameos came in words as well as pictures:

> In one spot in the mud at the side of the Canal road lay two British Tommies. They had been laid out ready for some transport to take them away. Standing beside them were three French girls, all dressed up, silk stockings and crimped hair. There they were, standing over the dead Tommies, asking if you would not like 'a little love'.

Orpen's soldiers did not scorn a little love. Goodbye-ee is as affecting a depiction as any of a parting. Some of his soldiers are tough and heroic, like the Grenadier Guards Sergeant and the Highlander Resting, or playful, as in the Christmas Night Dance. There is also the Lone Man with a Cigarette.

Opposite: *Skeleton in a Trench*, Sir William Orpen.

General Birdwood returning to his Headquarters, Sir William Orpen.

Thiepval, Sir William Orpen.

The End of a Hero and a Tank at Courcelette, Sir William Orpen.

Opposite: *'Good-bye-ee'*, Sir William Orpen.

Grenadier Guardsman, Sir William Orpen.

Opposite: *Man with a Cigarette*, Sir William Orpen.

Blown Up, Sir William Orpen.

Highlander passing a grave, Sir William Orpen.

Arthur Rhys Davids, Sir William Orpen.

But in the end, the image of these last days which Orpen seems to leave most powerfully is simply titled Blown Up.

The artist poet David Jones wrote in his *In Parenthesis* about how in the last years of war 'things hardened into a more relentless mechanical affair, took on a more sinister aspect, leading to the wholesale slaughter of the later years.' The emigrée Russian writer Irene Nemirovsky noted how these changes affected even the civilians in Paris in the last months of the war:

> Everything seemed strange, distorted, out of joint. This war no longer resembled the one that began in 1914. With its tanks, planes and armoured vehicles, with its soldiers in gas masks, this was nothing more than war on an industrial scale, an enormous company that traded in serial massacres, death on a production line.

Indeed, the final road to the Germans suing for peace was carved out by the new machines, aircraft as well as tanks, along with the arrival of half a million Americans.

The aircraft swirling above the troops in the sky almost immediately created wonder and heroes, like Lieutenant A. P. S. Rhys Davids, with his DSO and MC, whom Orpen painted before he was killed in action.

But the tanks in the paintings of the last months of the war have, by contrast, the sinister, inhuman aspect which Jones recognized. The crews are unseen, locked away inside. Their progress seems unguided by any human hand, and their crews died inside them, but they were crucial to the last months of Allied progress which were to end the war.

On the day when the Battle of Amiens began, the British and French had more than 2,000 aircraft, including fighters, bombers and reconnaissance planes, compared with fewer than 400 German machines. They had more than 300 of the latest type of tank, along with 100 of the lighter Whippet tanks.

The day saw past and future military technology intertwined. One tank commander reported seeing the Australian cavalry pursuing the fleeing enemy at the point of the sabre, while he was driving at more than 8mph down the road and accounting for other Germans with his Lewis guns. But the Germans had produced the first land mines, with ground level triggers, which could destroy even tanks.

During these last attacks across the whole front, the first ever air-drop of food rations was used to supply forward troops, and collapsible boats from the cross-Channel ferries were used to ford the canals, along with inflatable lifebelts. Much of the fighting, however, was still hand-to-hand with bayonets.

The American commander John Pershing's troops, pushing the Germans back in the last month of the war, provoked an amazed account from the official historian:

The campaign was a matter of thousands of obscure adventures of strangely picturesque heroism. It was jungle fighting, complicated by all the ghastly defences of ambushes and traps that modern science can devise – stagnant pools of poison gas, trip and pressure mines, log barricades and fields of wire entanglements, wolf pits, aerial torpedoes, tunnels, and the ubiquitous machine gun redoubts. For the most part the infantry had to work forward with its own power, exploring, skirmishing, and continually inventing on the spot novel ways of circumventing the innumerable works on which the enemy had spent the labour and thought of four years. The Argonne fighting suited the American temperament. It was a combination of pioneer work and Red Indian warfare, and there were Red Indians engaged in it who could work their way through brushwood almost as silently as a snake – a priceless thing in the dog fights in the forest.

Then, in the first days of November, came the news that the Germans were seeking a ceasefire. Foch's personal railway carriage was waiting in a siding near Compiègne.

Chapter Six

Ceasefire at Compiègne

Although there were some official photographs of the scene inside the Compiègne railway carriage, this seems to be the only painting that has survived. It shows Foch and the French General Weygand beside the British naval officers, Admiral Wemyss and (on his right) Rear Admiral George Hope, with the staff Captain Jack Marriott. The head of the German delegation, Matthias Erzberger, is standing opposite Foch with (on his left) General von Winterfeldt, Count von Oberndorff and Admiral Vanselow.

It was Vanselow who, when he heard that the German fleet was to be surrendered, said plaintively, 'But our Navy has not been defeated.'

To this Admiral Wemyss responded, 'It has only to come out! '

General von Winterfeldt had been included because he had worked with the French before the war, and it was thought he might be better received by the French negotiators. He had, five years earlier, actually been presented with the French Legion of Honour and was wearing the ribbon when the Germans were brought into the railway carriage. Foch looked at him and said, 'You have my permission not to wear that.'

The German delegates had already had a gruelling journey before they found themselves in Foch's railway carriage, having crossed the front line, under white flags, in five cars, near La Capelle. The French seem to have been determined that they should see the devastation which their armies had left behind them, and they were given a ten-hour tour of the battlefields before they were finally put on board a train and taken to the forest of Compiègne, north of Paris, where Foch in his own railway carriage was waiting.

Foch curtly asked them what they wanted, and then left his lieutenants and his Allies to convey the French and British demands. These were a lot more severe than the Fourteen Points which President Wilson had spelt out ten months earlier and were what the Germans were hoping for.

Indeed, the proposed terms were precise, severe and unequivocal. The Germans would have fourteen days to evacuate France, Belgium, Luxembourg and Alsace Lorraine. Any troops that were still there when the fortnight elapsed would be treated as prisoners of war.

They were to surrender, in addition to the fleet, 2,000 aircraft, 2,500 heavy guns and 2,500 field guns, to be handed over where they stood, along with 30,000 machine guns.

The Allies were to occupy the Rhine crossings at Cologne and Coblenz, and the Germans would have a month to evacuate their troops from everywhere within 6 miles of the river.

The Allies then required the surrender of huge quantities of railway equipment – the very means which had allowed the Germans to move their armies about so quickly and effectively

The Armistice, Compiègne railway carriage, Maurice Pillard Verneuil.

in the previous four years. Five thousand locomotives were required to be surrendered, and the same number of lorries. All German shipping in the Belgian ports was to be handed over. All Allied prisoners of war were to be immediately repatriated

There were attempts to negotiate, which were dismissed by the Allied side. But the German representatives protested that they did not have the authority to sign, so one of their staff officers, Count von Helldorff, was sent off to take the terms back to Germany. He was delayed when his own front line would not accept the white flag, but the terms eventually reached the newly installed socialist Prime Minister, Friedrich Ebert. By now Ludendorff had fled to Sweden, and it was left to Hindenburg to tell Ebert that the Army had collapsed and a ceasefire was essential. So, on 10 November, Ebert instructed Erzberger to sign, which he did at 5.00 am the next morning. The Armistice was to take effect six hours later at 11 o'clock.

The ceasefire was to cover hostilities all round the globe, from Romania to East Africa. The Germans were also required, rather optimistically, to hand back all the gold they had seized from conquered territories. Though the document was signed, and much of the seizure of equipment began within days or even hours, there was a strong element in Germany which wanted to disown the Compiègne deal. Indeed, there were outbreaks of fighting on the eastern frontier, with Hindenburg actually putting together an army group and attacking the Poles around Danzig. There was a series of meetings to try and nail down the details of the Armistice, the Germans claiming, for example, that they simply didn't possess the number of aeroplanes they were supposed to surrender.

Foch began to prepare the Allied armies for the possibility that they might have to resume the war and occupy Germany, and it was to be more than three months before a definitive Armistice was signed at Trèves on 16 February 1919.

Moreover, the Germans who had signed the Compiègne document were to return home to find themselves vilified by fervent nationalists. There was already talk of the 'stab in the back' by the politicians. They were ultimately to be branded 'the November criminals' and subjected to violent abuse in the conservative Press.

Erzberger was to hold a number of posts in the Weimar governments, but in 1921, when he was out walking in the Black Forest, he was shot dead by two naval officers, who then escaped to Hungary.

Count von Helldorf, who had been given the job of taking the Allied terms back through the lines to the German side, was eventually hanged in 1944 for his involvement in the July plot to assassinate Hitler.

Chapter Seven

Armistice Day

William Orpen was in Amiens on Armistice Day but he knew nothing of it, although he had heard that the Kaiser had abdicated the previous day. Around 11.00 am there was a burst of anti-aircraft firing, but Orpen, looking out of his hotel window, could see no sign of a German aircraft. He recalled thinking it must have been very high in the sky. Then, ten minutes later, there was a burst of cheering, and he realized the war was over.

Looking down into the hotel courtyard, he saw a serving girl he knew, Marthe, with her apron to her face, sobbing bitterly. He asked his landlady Marie-Louise what the matter was. 'It is the day that has upset her,' she said. 'You see her husband will come out of the trenches now, and come back to her.'

Orpen was to paint as ebullient a picture of that night's celebrations in Amiens as any of the portraits of celebration around the world. But he was acutely aware of the fears and sorrows which peace also brought.

The Amiens Armistice picture, though, is unalloyed excitement and delight. The searchlights act as spotlights illuminating the bannered and boisterous crowd. A kilted Scottish piper plays. A soldier kisses his girlfriend. There are pierrots and dancers and the palm leaves of peace.

Another painting of that night is a spirited lampoon, The Official Entry of the Kaiser, in which the citizens salute a pantomime donkey as it leads a dog in the Kaiser's cloak into the town.

But Orpen was in reflective mood:

On this day, looked forward to for years, I must admit that, studying people, I found something wrong. Peace was too great a thing to think about, the longing for it was too real, too intense. The fighting man – that marvellous thing that I had worshipped all the time I had been in France – had ceased actively to exist.

The one thing these wonderful super-men gave me to think was: What shall we do? Will they do as they promised for us? I gave up all my life and work at home and came out here to kill or be killed. Here I am stranded – I cannot kill any more and nobody wants to kill me. What am I to do?

Wending my way home through the blackened streets that night, I met a Tommy who threatened to kill me because of his misery. I talked him down and brought him to my room, and told him I really believed he would have a great time in the future. I doubted what I said, but he believed me, and went off to his billet happy for that one night.

Opposite: *Armistice Night in Amiens*, Sir William Orpen.

The cauldron of emotions portrayed by Orpen at the news of the ceasefire was mirrored throughout the Allied armies.

David Bilton, in his definitive account of the Hull Pals battalions, notes that the Pals had been engaged in forcing German troops back only the day before, with German deserters giving themselves up from the cellars of the town of Renaix; but the Pals also encountered bursts of machine gun fire from more determined elements of the enemy. The news of the ceasefire is recorded as being received by the Battalion at 2.00 in the morning – three hours before the Armistice was in fact signed. Private Aust recalled: 'We were sleeping in a cowshed when a sentry shouted in, "Eh lads. The war's over." The only response was from someone who crashed a heavy object against the door, and everyone slept again.'

Back in Hull, the city erupted in celebration, like all the cities of the Empire. But for all the joy and relief, there were dreadful pangs still to come.

Peace was already twelve days old when the mother of Lieutenant Whittington-Ince of the East Yorkshires received a letter from the Military Secretary telling her that her son had died on Armistice Day itself.

For the Pals, it was to be six months before they experienced their final homecoming and marched through the streets of Hull in a farewell parade up to Paragon Square. In those intervening months, detained in France, they had shared in the general discontent about the slow and apparently irrational process of demobilization. They had even been sent, armed, to suppress a mutiny amongst Allied troops at St Omer, sparked by the policy of sending some of the newest recruits home first and prioritizing men who claimed to have a job at home to go to.

Opposite: *Official Entry of the Kaiser*, Sir William Orpen.

Canadian Foresters, Sir Alfred Munnings.

Chapter Eight

Untouched Country

Alfred Munnings had been sent to France at the beginning of 1918 as an official artist with the Canadian cavalry. He was to paint the momentous picture of Flowerdew leading the charge of the Canadian cavalry at Moreuil, as well as a celebrated picture of their commander, General Jack Seely, riding his horse Warrior. After the war, Warrior was to become perhaps the most famous equine veteran of all, going home to the Isle of Wight to win the local point-to-point and becoming the hero of Seely's best-selling book, *My Horse Warrior*.

Munnings also painted pictures of the Canadian troops on the march, resting and watering their horses. But he was, uniquely, to become the artist who most affectingly portrayed the extraordinary serenity and bucolic bliss which, even after four years of war, lay behind the lines of devastation in rural France. In the summer of 1918, as the Allied armies surged forward towards the German border, Munnings allowed himself effectively to be kidnapped by the officers of the Canadian Forestry Corps, who had been sent over to acquire and cut timber for the trenches and the front line fortifications. 'I started afresh on another adventure,' he wrote. 'An adventure which had no danger and no risks, and which took me into some beautiful parts of France.'

This is the context of the paintings of the Forest of Dreux in Normandy – the foresters and their horses and the undisturbed woodland idyll. The new 'adventure' began with a memorable lunch at the Grand Hotel in Evreux, with its 'window boxes full of bright flowers'. Then 'suffused with the afterglow of food and wine, we went to the cathedral, and then on to one of those French government studs. We saw strength, beauty and movement combined in the Percheron horses, a row of great dappled hindquarters. '

Munnings was then taken down to the forest, where he painted an enormous oak tree – 'it was on a perfect day in the most divine sunlight. I painted a French sentry in his blue uniform, seated on the giant trunk.'

He went on to the forest of Bellême – 'These Canadian lumbermen were grand fellows. Their speech, dress, cast of countenance and expression, belonged to the illimitable forest spaces of Canada.' Munnings painted them building sawmills and felling trees, with 'a pale blue lake as my distant background'.

Their work was part of the gargantuan effort required to provide the wood for the trenches which stretched across France to the Swiss border. Labourers from all over the world had been recruited to dig and maintain these immense earthworks – more than 100,000 came from China alone.

Munnings then found himself swept up by Rowland Hill, the correspondent of the *Montreal Star*. Resplendent 'in one of those fine Cadillac cars, driven by a good chauffeur', they progressed across France via Dijon, all the way to the Jura hills and the border with Switzerland. 'I had little dreamed of such towns, surrounded by vineyards on hillsides, overlooking deep valleys. I was taken to Stendhal's country, to Besançon, and Ornans, the birthplace of Courbet.' He fondly recalled a 15-kilometre walk around a lake at Malbuison:

> I sat in the garden of an inn, watching the children who had come home from school, driving herds of cows, from each farm in the village street, to pastures surrounding the lake below. Following them on the curving road beside the lake, listening to the sweet sound of the cowbells, as twilight fell and mists rose from the lake, I became quite sentimental.

In all the pictures of the last days of the war, Munnings' record of rural France, still, in late 1918, unscarred by war, has a special, unique echo.

Chapter Nine

Peace in London

The English artist Caroline Beatrice Richardson produced more than a dozen watercolour pictures of Armistice Day in London. Born in Bengal, the daughter of a British naval surgeon, she was already an established painter when war broke out. She served as a nurse and made a large number of drawings of the wounded soldiers she encountered. On Armistice Day she produced a series of pictures which reflect the lightness and relieved emotion of the crowds, an atmosphere which was echoed in the vivid written accounts of that extraordinary day. This was an American correspondent's report:

The news of the signing of the armistice was given out by Premier Lloyd George to the papers a little before 11 o'clock on Monday, November 11. Up to that time London had preserved its usual phlegmatic calm. The successive announcements, in the closing days of the war, that Turkey had succumbed, that Austria had sent up the white flag, that the Kaiser had abdicated, and finally that Germany had sent its representatives to General Foch to arrange for a suspension of hostilities – all failed to disturb the Londoner in the pursuit of his established and historic routine. Apparently everything was coming out as England expected, and there was nothing to do but await events. The crash of empires and the fall of dynasties were the mere incidents of an arranged schedule.

The armistice was signed at 5 o'clock in the morning. London and England should have been notified of the result early on the day, immediately after the signing of the document. But the London evening papers are poor contraptions, and they have a way here of awaiting official announcements. It isn't news until the King, or the Premier, or some other great man has said it or done it. Or perhaps the censor was still on the job. In any event, the method of communicating to the public the great fact that Germany had officially acknowledged that it had lost, was through Lloyd George.

The day was threatening and misty; a very poor time for a public celebration of any kind. Then a lorry came lumbering up the Strand firing anti-aircraft guns. The significance of the exploit was not at first clearly understood. Some thought it was a final German air raid. But at last it dawned on the London mind that the war was over; and the impossible happened. London cast all reserve to the winds and let itself loose in a spontaneous and mighty demonstration. It was mainly a thing of moving and joyous crowds, going somewhere, anywhere, and making a noise – not a din after the American fashion, but yet a fairly noisy noise, all quite seemly, disciplined and respectable.

Pall Mall with St Martin-in-the-Fields in the background, Caroline Beatrice Richardson.

Cenotaph, Caroline Beatrice Richardson.

London is not yet thoroughly up in the art of getting the most out of a tin horn or a cow-bell. But the crowds, the crowds were enormous, and they were everywhere. It is said that London has 7,000,000 people. It must be an underestimate. Far more than that number apparently assembled at Trafalgar Square and before Buckingham Palace, and marched in platoons or companies or irregular regimental formations up and down the Strand. Or perhaps it was the same millions going in turn to all these common meeting places.

The crowd before the palace wanted to see and hear the King and Queen. That royal lady has a very large place in the calculations of the English people. 'We want King George!' cried the people. The thoughts of more than one American went back to memorable and unexampled scenes in Chicago in 1912, when uproarious throngs insistently proclaimed 'We want Roosevelt!'

There the very air was tense with the electric fervour of irrepressible feeling loudly and vehemently expressed. Here, where they have King George, and evidently intend to keep him, there was no emotional outburst, no passionate outcry, no mob frenzy, merely the more or less formal call of a disciplined people to see their King, doubtless because they reasoned among themselves, in good English style, that it was the correct procedure in the circumstances. There is no denying the popularity of the King, however. If they were to hold an election for King in England tomorrow, the incumbent would distance all others at the polls.

At a quarter to 11 there were no signs of special commotion before the palace. A few idlers had gathered to watch the ceremony of changing the guard. The only flag in sight was the royal standard. At 11 o'clock, precisely, a typewritten copy of the Premier's announcement that hostilities had ceased was hung outside the railings and then the maroons exploded. The crowds began to gather, coming from all directions like bees in a swarm. Many had flags. Men on horseback came from somewhere and reined up before the palace. Taxicabs and motor cars came along and people who wanted to see better began to climb on the roofs. Within a few minutes many thousands had assembled and they began to call for the King.

At 11:15 King George, in the uniform of an Admiral, appeared on the balcony. The Queen, bareheaded and wearing a fur coat, was with him. The Duke of Connaught came too, and the Princess Mary. The soldiers presented arms and the Irish Guards band played the national anthem and the crowd solemnly took up the slow refrain. Then the band played 'Rule Britannia'. The people sang again and flags began to wave. They were nearly all British flags. The King removed his cap and his loyal subjects cheered, and someone proposed a groan for the Kaiser, which was given sonorously, and the ruler of Great Britain and all the Indies donned his cap and the royal group went back into the palace.

The throngs, pleased and decorously animated, moved away, but their places were taken by other thousands, and the whole performance was repeated. At one of his appearances the King was graciously inspired to make a speech. It consisted of only a sentence or two, but it was all right and the people applauded rapturously.

Later, the King decided to drive through the city. He was accompanied by the Queen and the Princess Mary. Rain was falling, but nobody in England minds rain. It was a triumphal procession. Everywhere at central points had gathered many thousands to welcome their majesties. One mighty group was at Victoria Memorial; another at Admiralty Arch; another at Ludgate Circus; and still another at Mansion House, where the Lord Mayor, in his official robes of black and gold, was on hand to receive the royal pair.

The streets were encompassed all the way by many people. Here and there was a police officer, but the police had no difficulty with the crowds. There was no special or unusual guard for the King and Queen, only a few outriders. They have no fear, evidently, in England, that anything untoward will happen to the Crown, through the act of a madman, or the deliberate deed of a regicide. A policeman's baton is enough.

On the succeeding day it was announced that the King and Queen would attend a thanksgiving service at St Paul's Cathedral. The street scenes of the previous day were repeated during the progress of the royal couple to the magnificent centre of worship. It is a noble and wonderful shrine, with a fit setting for occasions of vast importance. Great bells rang and a mighty concourse gathered, and a solemn and beautiful ceremony was conducted in commemoration of the triumph of the allied cause.

The Strand, ending in Trafalgar Square, the heart of London, is the most popular thoroughfare in the city. It attracts the visiting soldiers, and the soldiers make up a great part of the ordinary moving crowds.

When the joy-making began, the crowds took possession not only of the Strand, but of all available vehicles. A favourite adventure of men and women was to commandeer a taxicab and to pile in and on anywhere, preferably on top. One car, with a prescribed capacity for four, had exactly twenty-seven persons sardined in its not-too-ample proportions. Then there were lorries – automobile trucks – crowded with soldiers, civilians and girls, all waving flags and singing or shouting.

Soldiers formed in procession and marched along. After a while they turned about and went the other way. Girls in uniform – munitions workers – appeared in large numbers, and walked along, arm-in-arm with the men in khaki. Flags were plentiful, mostly British, with a fair proportion of American, French and Belgian. But the unvarnished truth is that Britain was celebrating a British victory. Well, why not? They were polite enough to make reasonable concessions to their allies – whenever they thought of it.

A group of Americans standing on the walk, somewhat uncertainly displaying American flags, were frequently cheered by passing revellers. Once a lot of Canadians came in sight, and some of them broke from their fellows, and came over and asked the Americans for the flags, which were promptly given them.

At another time, a great lorry with perhaps 50 passengers aboard, stopped in front of an American with a bandaged head, waving Old Glory, and gave him three rousing cheers. They thought, doubtless that he was a hero of the war, with a wound honourably won in battle. He did not undeceive them. The day went on with no diminution of the crowds or moderation of the excitement. Apparently it increased rather than diminished. Business was wholly suspended, except in the restaurants and hotels, and the metropolis gave itself up to merry-making. Yet it was mainly an unorganized, though orderly, spectacle of movement, without incidents.

There was little drinking or drunkenness, apparently, in the streets, though there was plenty, and to spare, later in the great hotels. Possibly the crowd was sober because intoxication costs money nowadays in England; or perhaps it was not in the humour to drink. But the gay assemblies within the walls of the restaurants had no such scruples. There was much drinking, much noise, much laxity, a complete departure from the innocent gaiety of the streets.

The celebration did not end on Monday night. But it started up again on Tuesday and continued through the week. When London celebrates it celebrates. There is no question about it. Occasionally the crowd broke bounds. At Piccadilly Circus there was a great bonfire made up of big signboards taken by force from passing omnibuses. The same thing occurred at Trafalgar Square, where the effort to subdue the flames by water from a firemen's hose led to cracking the stones at the foundation of the Nelson monument, making a serious disfigurement of that splendid column.

Chapter Ten

Peace in North America

The joyous celebrations were worldwide, as the news crossed the time zones. George Luks was a Philadelphia artist and newspaperman. His picture is an exuberant splash of flags and faces, against the smoke of fireworks, recording a day to which the *Philadelphia Evening Ledger* saluted as follows:

CITY THRONGS IN MIGHTIEST CELEBRATION

Just one great, big, glorious victory parade.

That was Philadelphia today.

There was a parade every minute – everywhere. They started with the dawn. Who knows when they will finish?

This was declared an official holiday for the entire State, by Governor Brumbaugh. But there was no waiting for any official declaration. The first factory whistle proclaiming peace proclaimed also a holiday.

Business was suspended. The Stock Exchange was idle. Stores, big and little closed their doors. The mills shut down. The shipyards stopped work. All poured their countless happy thousands into the centre of the city.

The municipal parade, arranged by Mayor Smith, and with the Mayor at its head, was officially the big event of the day; but this was only one of many hundred such demonstrations.

Everybody paraded. Ponderous gentlemen from the Union League marched gaily. The Oyster Shell Social was represented. Shop girls marched. Girl munition workers, in their uniforms, paraded. Soldiers, sailors, lawyers, merchants oh, everybody! Such a day!

Broad, Chestnut and Market streets were the main-travelled highways for these cheering, shouting, bright-faced thousands, who carried bells and waved flags and blew horns and danced in their glee. And bands! A million! Count them yourself.

Independence Square, with its old State House and sacred Liberty Bell, was one of the focal points for the celebrants. The Liberty Statue at City Hall was another. But all through the city, in all communities, in all suburbs, the revelry went on in the bright, mild sunshine of this greatest day of modern history.

The celebration had its serious side. The churches, many of them, were thrown open for thankful devotion. And many thousands dropped to their knees for a prayer of gratitude.

What a day! The wonder of it! The glory of it! Never to be forgotten.

Armistice Night, 1918, in *Philadelphia*, George Luks.

Armistice Day, 1918, in New York, Gifford Reynolds Beal.

In New York, Gifford Beal was on hand to paint the scene which the newspaper described:

The glooms who said that New York had exhausted its reserves of enthusiasm when the false report of the coming of peace was spread abroad last week by the United Press were wrong. Notwithstanding last Thursday's tremendous celebration, there was enough emotion left, when the real and authentic news of the signing of the armistice arrived before daylight yesterday morning, to start a celebration that lasted without interruption for fully twenty-four hours, and while it was going on stopped all kinds of business in the city except theatrical performances and the dispensing at retail of food.

Yet it was not altogether the same kind of celebration that occurred last week here. Ever since the false news came last Thursday, New York had been looking for the real news of the end of the war at almost any hour, and constant expectancy had taken some of the edge off the tidings. Moreover, there was no longer the pressure that was behind the unprecedented scenes last week; that very celebration had let off much of the surplus steam, and nothing else could quite get up the enthusiasm which was then manifested. Last week, when the false peace report dropped suddenly, as if out of the skies, on a city which had not expected the news at that particular moment. New York was like a city which found itself saved after entertaining gloomy forebodings. On every countenance in the street, in the early hours of that day before the peace report was known to be false, there was a heartfelt, unconscious smile of rapture, an outward token of the coming to every man and woman of glad tidings of great joy. The devil was dead and everybody felt a particular personal interest in his demise.

Yesterday this first spontaneous expression of relief had already been discounted; there was more of a prearranged air about the celebration. But if it was deliberate, it was none the less heartfelt, none the less of universal appeal. The whole city joined in celebrating the final and complete disappearance of German autocracy, a disappearance whose surprising fullness was not known when the false peace report came last week. And so, while there was not the impressive revelation of a people's soul which was evoked by the false news of Thursday, there was none the less a celebration which the city of New York will hold in its memory for many years.

A man who learned late of last Thursday night that the United Press story was inaccurate, and that the armistice had not been signed, remarked to his friends: 'Well, they're going to sign it pretty soon, and I'll just keep on celebrating until they do.' There were many like him, and it was some of these determined jubilators, sitting up all night in order not to miss any piece of news that might arrive between sunset and sunrise, who got the first tidings that the war was really over. Around the newspaper offices, when the news first came in at 3 o'clock yesterday morning, and at the naval offices on the tip of the island, the story that the war was over was first spread; and from Times Square, Park Row, and Battery Park it soon spread all over the city.

Nocturnal revellers going home and sober night workers eating breakfast in the restaurants, were the first who heard the news shouted by the newsboys in Times Square as they ran out with the late editions telling of the signing of the armistice. From uptown and downtown a crowd presently collected to read the bulletins, to get the extras, and to stare up at the great searchlight on the Times Building, which was flashing the news over all the city. That searchlight shone into the windows of hotels and apartment houses and woke sleepers, who had not expected the news to come at such an hour, but who were ready to get up and celebrate whenever it came.

In a few minutes the sirens that were installed to give warning of an air raid, but that are hardly likely ever to be used for that purpose, started up once more to send that glad news over the city. They assailed the heavens with their clamorous blare, and presently other whistles and church bells, too, joined in a tumult of noise. Downtown at the Barge Office, where the Naval Reserve officers have their headquarters, buglers were sent out on the roof to blow a fanfare of triumph, and elsewhere local noisemakers hurried out into the open to help in raising the clamor. Right and left persons who were sleeping peacefully before the blue dawn of Monday morning stirred uneasily, sat up in bed, and then realised what it all meant.

Many children went to school yesterday morning, but many others did not. The principals and teachers, looking over those who had come, and feeling the thrill of the great day within themselves, dismissed almost everyone as soon as the opening exercises were over. So by 9.30 o'clock the streets were full of boys and girls with armloads of books, who had nothing before them but the patriotic duty of making it as big a day as possible. Many office workers communicated with their employers by telephone, or with the offices where their employers should have been and weren't; and thus learned that there would be no work on the day that saw the end of the biggest war of all history.

The Governors of the Stock Exchange got together before the hour for the regular opening and decided not to open at all. The other Exchanges followed their example, and most offices realised that but little work could be got out of anybody who was imbued with the spirit of celebration.

In the factories of the city most of the workers reported as usual and obtained a day off as soon as they had checked in. And the closing of schools and factories almost as soon as they opened brought about the development of the principal feature of the morning celebration – the parades of school children and factory employees, which swept up and down Fifth Avenue till past noon, from friendly rivalry of display of banners and in competing uproars of noise.

After a brief address at the Plaza by Professor Thomas G. Masaryk, President of the Czechoslovak National Committee, the bell, which is a replica of the original Liberty Bell and was first rung at the Declaration of the Independence of the oppressed nationalities in Philadelphia two or three weeks ago, was taken down the avenue in procession and then through the districts of the east side where Czechoslovak and Polish population is strongest.

Just to make it a real Liberty Day, Judge Malone of General Sessions, before adjourning yesterday morning, suspended sentence on thirteen young men who had pleaded guilty to minor offences and had been sentenced to indeterminate periods in the penitentiary. 'Today,' said Judge Malone, 'is the dawn of the world's rebirth, and it is a time when all men should begin their lives anew and dedicate themselves to those ideals which have been so gloriously vindicated on the battlefields of France, I suspend all these sentences during good behaviour.'

The Fifth Avenue Association gave a Victory Luncheon to representatives of the allied nations at the Ritz-Carlton. The party, escorted by a detail from the 22nd Regular Infantry from Governors Island and carrying flags of all the allied countries, paraded up and down the avenue before the event.

The Salvation Army held a formal thanksgiving celebration early in the morning on the steps of the Public Library at Fifth Avenue and Forty-Second Street. As soon as the news of the signing of the armistice was received at the headquarters on Fourteenth Street the officers began collecting their workers by telephone, and soon after sunrise some 100 of them were on hand. Headed by the army's band, behind which marched a double platoon of war workers just back from service in France to help in the United War Work campaign, and another double platoon of workers about to sail, the party marched up the avenue to the Public Library, with Commander Evangeline Booth leading the main body of the procession. On the library steps the entire body knelt in thankful prayer, while the crowds around stood with bared heads; and when the devotional exercises were over there was a wild outburst of cheers, followed by an address in which Commander Booth set forth the needs of the army for the campaign.

With the closing of factories and offices, many motor trucks were commandeered for purposes of display, and, crowded with horn-blowing, bell-ringing employees of the firm to which the truck belonged, often draped with bunting and banners bearing legends expressive of the sentiment of the day, they drove up and down through the principal streets of Manhattan with shrieking horns, scattering the crowds ahead of them, but miraculously escaping accidents somehow.

Hastily formed parades of workers marched up and down, with commercialism and patriotism artfully blended on their banners; a procession of garment workers bore at the head the name of their firm, and behind it a banner reading: 'We made the clothes worn by the boys who canned the Kaiser.' A broom factory sent out a battalion of workmen whose procession carried at its head the banner: 'We made the broom that swept the Hohenzollern away.'

The procession of city employees which Mayor Hylan had ordered for last Thursday night, before learning that the report of the armistice was false, was held yesterday, starting from Lafayette and Canal Streets. It had been intended originally to start from the City Hall but the crowd there was so dense that Mayor Hylan eventually decided to start it further uptown. Meanwhile thousands were waiting around the front of the City Hall, and much attention was attracted by a gray-haired negro who sat weeping on the steps of the building. He said that he had been born a slave on a Virginia plantation, and that he had given to the country that had made him free, two sons who had been killed in France.

Mayor Hylan himself, with Mrs Hylan by his side, headed the municipal parade when it finally got under way, with his secretary, Grover Whalens and Police Lieutenant William Kennell just behind him. Every department was headed by its own band as the parade, including thousands of city employees, marched up Lafayette Street and Fourth, then across to Fifth Avenue, to the avenue to Forty-second Street across to Broadway, and up to Columbus Circle, where the Mayor dropped out and reviewed the parade before it dispersed. Police Commissioner Richard Enright marched at the head of the Commissioners.

The Post Office employees, headed by their own band and marching several thousand strong had intended to join the city officials' parade but eventually they got tired of waiting in their station around the old Post Office at Broadway and Park Row, and after marching past the City Hall to be reviewed by the Mayor, they marched uptown to the new Post Office at Eighth Avenue and Thirty-third Street.

The courts closed as soon as they opened yesterday, after a few words from the Judges relative to the significance of the day. Judge William Wadhams, who had read of the Kaiser's flight to Holland, directed the clerk of the court to issue a bench warrant for his arrest.

Up in the Bronx they had a parade of special interest to several thousand citizens. Eight hundred men from eleven draft districts had been ordered to entrain yesterday morning for Fort Wright near New Haven, Conn. Their relatives and friends came out to see them off, the usual festivities attending a parade of drafted men, in this case enlivened by the collapse of German resistance and the certainty that those now called up for service would merely aid in sweeping up the pieces. But it appeared that not even that much would fall to their share; when they reached the Grand Central Station, where they were to take trains for the training camp, they were met by a representative of Martin Conboy, local director of the draft, who told them that in view of the signing of the armistice, draft orders had been countermanded and they could go back home. Whereupon there were shortly 800 active enthusiasts added to the crowds that were celebrating in the Bronx.

Czechoslovak and Polish soldiers, some in the horizon blue of the independent armies of those nations in France, and others wearing the khaki of the American forces, guarded the new Liberty Bell of the Democratic Mid-European Union, the organization of the newly freed nations of Central and Eastern Europe, on a parade down Fifth Avenue.

The National Board of Fire Underwriters saw danger in this littering of the street inches deep with inflammable material and issued the following warning:

Last Thursday when the streets, roofs, and window ledges of the city were carpeted with tons of waste paper, running in depth of from two inches to two feet in celebrating the reported German surrender, New York was in perhaps greater danger from a conflagration than ever before in its history. There is the danger today that this hazard will again be created, as the paper-throwing habit is once more in evidence.

Fire Chief Kenlon expresses himself as keenly troubled by the possibilities of this condition. With the streets crowded with people many of whom are smokers and give small heed to the disposition of their lighted matches and cigar and cigarette ends, a conflagration is imminent. In addition, the numerous automobiles filled with gasoline and grease may easily set fire to the paper on the streets through muffler backfires. Chief Kenlon declares that if a blaze starts under such conditions it may easily sweep the lower end of Manhattan and cause the loss of thousands of lives as well as of millions of dollars' worth of property.

But despite the risk and the fact that many fire engines were out on the curb and in use most of the day as whistling machines, there was no fire of any consequence.

The backfiring of automobiles to make a noise was once more a feature – indeed, it seems that this method of making a noise and the torn paper method of display are likely to become fixtures in New York's future celebrations.

One feature, however, which was present last week but is hardly likely to become permanent was the promiscuous kissing of soldiers and sailors by good-looking girls, which was in evidence on every street of the city yesterday. The soldier or sailor, whether of the United States or the Allies, who got through yesterday inosculate had only his own fleet-footedness to thank for it, for enthusiastic and comely young women were everywhere and displayed a vivacity which was the envy and despair of the disregarded civilians.

As on Thursday last, the former Kaiser was the object of most of the wit blazoned on the banners carried in procession or on the posters which adorned the windows of shops closed for the day. One motor truck carried a big tin can with the head of William Hohenzollern thrust out of its mouth and the inscription: 'We've got the Kaiser canned this time.' Another truck showed the Kaiser in a bag. In a window at Fifth Avenue and Thirty-Sixth Street there was a hurried sketch of the Kaiser pawning his crown which halted many a passerby, who stood and laughed as they reflected on the hurried exit of the recent war lord. Other signs in parades or windows read as follows:

He wanted the world and got the gate. Poor Bill. Rest in pieces.
'I'll stand no nonsense from America after the war.'
Who said work?
Me und Gott have dissolved partnership. Gott now manages the business.

Holland is full of Limburger – the biggest one ran away.
What did I tell you?
God made Wilson, but who made the Kaiser?

On a large map of Germany – 'Good farmland for sale. See W. Wilson, Washington.'

All in all, it would have been a gloomy day for the Kaiser.

Toward night the warships and camouflaged merchant vessels in the North River, which had been decked with flags all day, turned on all their lights and began to play their searchlights up and down Riverside Drive. The big apartment houses along the Drive were brilliantly illuminated. Far down the bay the Statue of Liberty was once more alight; the big double lamps along Fifth Avenue, one side of which had been dark to save coal during most of the war, were illuminated last night in celebration, and any lightless night regulations were cancelled for the time being. The airplanes which had flown across the city from time to time during the day had gone back to their nests on Long Island, but searchlights from the Times Building and other high edifices in the city, as well as from the anti-aircraft defences in the parks, played along the sky and swept now and then along the walls of apartment houses and hotels where the lights were gleaming in windows. For an impromptu illumination it was extraordinarily brilliant.

While many saloons were closed after sunset, many persons had become hilarious before the bars were shut up, and again, as last week, the regulations about selling liquor to soldiers and sailors were ignored, leading to actions on the part of some of them that brought grave criticism from the onlookers.

And yet, for all the drinking, and even drunkenness, there was but one serious outbreak – a fight between negroes and the police in Harlem. Late at night the celebration was like that of an election night. Such celebrations New York will see again, whether the world goes dry or not; but it will be a long time before this or any other city sees the like of the outpouring of spontaneous emotion which the false rumour of peace brought out last week and, which remained in considerable quantities when the real news came out yesterday.

For the Canadians, who had been committed to the war much longer than the Americans, the celebrations had a special intensity. Joseph Ernest Sampson painted the day of peace in Toronto. The Toronto newspaper reported the events of 12 November, but with thought, too, for those who would not return:

Citizens, Thrilled by News of Armistice, Throng the Down-Town Section, Hold Parades, Burn the Kaiser in Effigy, Start Bonfires, and Raise Greatest Racket Ever Heard Here.

Toronto never knew such revelry as has prevailed during the last 24 hours. Since the moment that the official word was received, between two and three o'clock yesterday morning, that the armistice was signed, business has been at a standstill, work has mattered not at all – the spirit of victory has gripped the people. It needed a Kipling to compose another Recessional or to call aloud to the multitude his familiar lines:

Lord God of Hosts
Be with us yet
Lest we forget.

Toronto came nearer to forgetting last night than ever before in the city's history, and yet the memory of the wonderful service in Queens Park the day before must have held those in restraint who would otherwise have become drunk with the sight of power. Yesterday Toronto thought only of the glory of having won. It spent itself in giving voice to pent-up feelings of pride in the achievement of the allies, the master stroke of Foch, backed by the generalship of the allied commanders, but it rent the air with shrieks and shouting for the gallantry of the Canadians, and the 66,000 odd men whom the city awaits to honor in person.

Premier Hearst announced: 'With a deep sense of gratitude to Almighty God and supreme pride and glory in the immortal achievements of our empire and its allies. Canadians have received the news that a victorious peace has been accomplished. The complete overthrow and defeat of German militarism and Hohenzollernism and all that they represent is the most glorious vindication of freedom the human race has ever known.'

Mayor Church said: 'Toronto has longed for such a day as this to come. The citizens may be proud of the noble, glorious and inspiring record it has made in the war. The memory of its war service will never fade. Mad militarism has been destroyed forever, and all the allies fought for has been won. Let us not forget what the mother country has done in this war. The British fleet has saved Canada and America from the awful horrors of war on our own soil. The mother country raised eight million men and nearly one million have given their lives in defence of liberty and civilization.'

Opposite: *Armistice Day, Toronto,* Joseph Sampson.

The paper printed a poem by Robert Todd:

The Town's Gone Wild

Come along, be merry, join our jubilee,
Mars has got the knock-out, Peace is in, you see.
Toot your little tooter, deck yourself with flags,
Grab your feather tickler, be among the wags.
Don't forget the powder, sprinkle it around,
Laugh – it will not hurt you; make you strong and sound.
Show you are a human – be just as a child,
Everybody's happy; the town's gone wild.
     Take your wife or sweetheart,
     Stroll on Yonge or Queen,
Million flags are waving; oh, what sights are seen!
Smiles, about ten million greet you everywhere,
Everybody's busy-busy chasing care.
Climb into an auto, choose a truck or Ford;
Blow your little whistle; what a din, Oh, Lord!
Peace, we bid you welcome, woman, man and child,
Everybody's happy, the town's gone wild.
Toronto, Canada.

The piece continued:

There Are Still Anxious Hearts in Canada

In spite of the general rejoicing, there are still many anxious hearts in Canada. Canadian soldiers were engaged in hard fighting up to the very moment that the armistice was signed, and indeed for some hours after. The last shot of the war seems to have been fired by a Canadian. This means that many Canadian soldier boys have been killed or wounded whose names have not yet appeared on the casualty lists.

In many cases fifteen, twenty or even thirty days elapse between a casualty and the receipt of the news from Ottawa by the next of kin. If we wait for the slow process of official reporting, thousands of parents, wives, sisters and sweethearts must pass the next two or three weeks in anxiety and gloom. Many soldiers, of course will cable home; but the lines are congested and many may be unable to send the cable.

The apprehensions of the *Toronto Globe* were to be only too justified. The actual ceasefire at 11.00 on the morning of 11 November seems to have been extraordinarily precisely observed. The war had become a conflict in which timing was crucial. Bombardments opened, attacks were launched from the trenches, to a very exact timetable, dictated by the Army commanders. Even the most junior officers had watches which were regularly checked and calibrated. Thus, across the hundreds of miles of trenches and fortifications from the English Channel to the Alps, the guns seem to have stopped firing, both German and Allied, within a matter of seconds of the agreed time. Indeed, some of the artillery officers encouraged their troops to line up holding a long lanyard attached to the firing mechanism, so that, all pulling it as the last seconds ticked away, they would be able to claim to have fired the last shot of the Great War.

But the five and a half hours between the actual signing of the Armistice in the Compiègne railway carriage and its implementation were still to see terrible losses. Though the news of the coming end of the fighting was flashed by cable and wireless across the world, and the Army commanders knew within an hour or two that the war was over, some took the view that their duty was to press on until the last moment.

In the United States, in particular, through the early weeks of 1919, and through to 1920, the families of men who, they were told, had died on 11 November began to piece together the story of the events of that morning, and it grew into a serious political scandal.

The morning of 11 November had originally been selected by Marshall Foch for another major push by the American forces, under General John Pershing; their objective was the capture of a railway line, which would then divide the retreating German Army. When the news came through of the Armistice, the order to attack was cancelled. But soon after, the cancellation itself was rescinded. The attack was on again, for 1035 hours.

There were sixteen American divisions involved. Their commanders were faced with an extraordinary dilemma. Some took the view that the order was the opportunity to inflict a last blow on the enemy and capture the objectives they had been advancing towards for the last few weeks. Others decided that they could not expose their men to the risk of death so shortly before the conflict was due to end. In the end, seven of the divisional commanders decided to press on, and three of the divisions, in crossing the heavily defended Meuse River, took more than 1,000 casualties, with 127 men being killed in the last hour or so before the whistles and the bugles announced the cessation of firing.

HMS Mantis on the Tigris, Donald Maxwell.

Chapter Eleven

Peace in the Middle East

In the Middle East, the war against the Turks had ended just a few weeks earlier. Donald Maxwell was an official artist with the Royal Navy, but also an intrepid traveller in Mesopotamia, both before and after the war. Aboard a variety of British ships he followed the chaotically retreating Turks as they fled up the Euphrates back towards Anatolia. He portrays a very different scene to the stern and stubborn resistance that the Turks had been putting up against General Allenby's forces in Palestine. In 1918 he found himself aboard a boat called the *Shushan*:

> This gallant little curiosity is no late-conscripted product of the war. She is one of the pukka ships of the Navy in Mesopotamia – one of the Old Contemptibles. Armed with a three-pounder which caused such havoc to her decks when fired that it is reported she had to be turned round after each round. Two shots in the same direction would have wrecked the vessel.

The comic episodes and droll insouciance of Maxwell and the Navy as they made their way past Kut to Baghdad were a sweet contrast to the events of only three years earlier, when the besieged British garrison at Kut had surrendered to the Turks, in arguably the greatest single British military disaster up to that time. General Townshend had given himself up, and thousands of his troops were forced to march through the desert to captivity, with thousands dying on the way. By 1918, however, Maxwell and the British sailors with him could afford to be almost flippant:

> The Turks had fled from Kurna and we were chasing them up the river with an amazing medley of craft, like a nightmare of Henley Regatta suddenly mobilised. The *Shushan* was in the forefront of the battle. Led by the sloops *Espiegle*, *Clio* and *Odin*, the Stunt Armada came to Ezra's Tomb at twilight. The river was high and the land in between the great bends was a maze of rushes and lagoons. Turkish hospital hulks, like Noah's arks, little steamers and loaded *mahailas* jostled each other in their endeavours to get up against the strong stream.
>
> Across the bend, some two or three miles away, the Turkish gunboat *Marmaris* with a little fleet of her own was putting on every ounce of fuel she had. Then our sloops opened fire and a desultory cannonade was kept up as it grew darker and darker. Our firing

The Navy at Baghdad, Donald Maxwell.

ceased, but we saw that the *Marmaris* had been set alight by her crew. But we captured the whole of the enemy's flotilla.

Maxwell went on to paint his satisfied picture of the British cruiser at Baghdad. He lingered there after the Turks succumbed, and the British troops, as he remarked, could talk only of demobilization and going home. In Baghdad he found 'streets through which beggars and British officers, camels and Ford cars, jostled each other in vain attempts to get on'.

But while the British and French were carving up the Middle East on paper in Paris, Maxwell found himself contemplating what the British would do with their newly conquered land – 'The natural assumption of every patriotic Briton is that the desert will immediately blossom as the rose.'

He did indeed catch glimpses of the Fertile Crescent – exceedingly beautiful – in the backwaters and channels of the Tigris and the Euphrates, but 'centuries of neglect and the blight of the unspeakable Turk have dealt hardly with this country. It will be many a long day before it is Paradise Regained.'

However, Maxwell also saw positive signs: 'Our army of occupation includes "irrigation officers" and gradually the work of watering the country is extending', although he could not imagine who was going to live there – 'Mesopotamia is not a white man's country.'

He was well aware of the oil fields around Basra and the Persian Gulf. He had been to Abadan and seen 'the two adventurous pipes which start courageously with crude oil and conduct it by or through every obstacle'. And he had learned the art of tightrope walking on the pipes to avoid the sand and mud. He had also seen the sunken hulks with which the Turks had vainly tried to halt the British Navy's progress.

By the time he left for home he possessed a guarded confidence that the British would make a success of what he regarded as their new possession.

Chapter Twelve

Peace in the Mediterranean

While Donald Maxwell was painting the ships of the Royal Navy in Baghdad itself, there was a consciousness that the times, though triumphant, were still nervous. Beyond Constantinople, in the Black Sea, the Russian fleet had been handed over to German control by the Bolsheviks after the Treaty of Brest-Litovsk. Somewhere in the Black Sea were eight battleships, twenty-four light cruisers and destroyers, a dozen submarines, even an aircraft carrier, the *Almaz*. And the German battle cruiser *Goeben* was also loose in these waters.

The British and French had gathered a considerable fleet off the Dardanelles, with four battleships, as well as cruisers and destroyers. They had put men ashore on the forlorn, and now deserted, beaches of Gallipoli. But there was no way of knowing whether the warships beyond the Straits represented any sort of threat.

These were the uncertain days in November, between the Ottomans acknowledging their defeat and the Germans accepting the Armistice on the other side of Europe. In the event, no opposition was offered as the Allied ships made their way up the Bosphorus and hove to, with the dome of Aya Sophia and the minarets of Constantinople in their sights.

The Ottoman Empire, overlords of the Middle East for more than 500 years, crumbled, in the end, in a matter of weeks. It fell to the Royal Navy to take their surrender and the artists Philip Connard and Frank Mason to paint their subjection in the most emphatic – indeed symbolic – fashion. Mason – one of the first official artists – had himself been an officer on a Royal Navy gunboat. A founder member of the celebrated Staithes group of artists on the Yorkshire coast, his wartime work took him to Egypt and through to the conclusion of the Turkish campaign, before he returned to London in time to portray the Armistice celebrations. His picture shows the mighty guns of HMS *Superb* pointing at Constantinople itself, Aya Sophia and the minarets under their domination. Philip Connard gives us the German cruiser *Goeben*, white flag of surrender flying, being dispatched past the German embassy, on the Bosphorus quayside, to captivity in the hands of the British Mediterranean fleet; and then HMS *Caesar* lowering her guns to point at the Golden Horn.

Four years earlier, the Ottoman Turks, inveigled into the war on the German side by astute diplomacy, had almost severed the most crucial link in the British Empire, the Suez Canal. More than 100,000 British soldiers had surrendered at Kut, in modern Iraq, unable to defend the vital oilfields from Turkish and Arab armies. There had then been the disastrous and failed attempt to break the Turks at Gallipoli

It had taken most of the next three years for the British, Australian and Indian troops and T. E. Lawrence's desert Arabs to slowly turn the tide. General Allenby had relentlessly forced the

The Surrender of the Goeben, Philip Connard.

Guns of HMS Caesar, Philip Connard.

Admiral Calthorpe, Philip Connard.

Turks back until, in October 1918, Damascus fell, and the route to Constantinople was open. Almost at the same time, the Turks and their Bulgarian allies on the other side of the Black Sea had been forced into capitulation.

The Royal Navy was now in total control of the eastern Mediterranean, with Admiral Calthorpe, the imposing figure in Connard's portrait, in command. The picture gives him his full title: Vice Admiral the Honourable Sir Somerset A. Gough-Calthorpe GCMG, KCB, CVO. To him, the Turks seeking peace had to present themselves.

Connard's paintings of the Royal Navy at Constantinople have all the aura of a Roman triumph – imperious captains, submissive captives, caparisoned conquerors. The guns of the great ship – named HMS *Caesar*, no less – look down on Aya Sophia and the Golden Horn. The *Goeben*, flying the white flag of humiliation, is being made to sail right past the German embassy and its staff.

While Allenby's British Empire troops were forcing their way from the Suez Canal up through Palestine to capture Jerusalem and Damascus, Allied troops in Salonika in northern Greece , under the French General d'Esperey, had launched an attack on Turkey's ally Bulgaria which had ended in the latter's capitulation. Meanwhile, the Turks were retreating rapidly from the oil fields of Mesopotamia.

The Turkish government, thus threatened with invasion and retreating on its eastern front, had become convinced that their only hope was to seek an armistice. They still held captive the British General Townshend, whose forces had succumbed three years earlier at Kut, and he was sent with a message to Admiral Gough-Calthorpe, whose ship, HMS *Agamemnon*, was in the bay of Mudros at the Greek island of Lemnos.

Calthorpe, instructed by the British Prime Minister Lloyd George, agreed to see a delegation headed by the Turkish Navy Minister Rauf Bey and imposed a 24-point armistice agreement on the Turks which included the option to occupy Constantinople. The Ottoman army and navy were also to be disbanded. The war in the Middle East thus came to an end, though there were to be years of discussion between the Allies, and a Turkish nationalist revolt, before the modern borders of the Middle East emerged.

Connard, having painted Admiral Calthorpe in his naval finery, was thus able to go with the fleet to Constantinople and depict this clear and decisive panorama of a defeated empire.

The Royal Navy's victorious arrival at Constantinople had been hard won. The Navy had been part of the over-ambitious and failed attempt to outflank the Turks in 1915 at Gallipoli, where it had devised imaginative means to land, not only troops but guns, ammunition, horses and their forage – then find ways of retrieving man and beast from the bloody debacle that the campaign became.

But then, despite the activities of some German submarines, and with the help of bases in Italy and Croatia, the Navy had slowly recovered command of the eastern Mediterranean. The straits of the Dardanelles and the Bosphorus, and the route to Constantinople, remained beyond them. But three German warships were at least bottled up in the Black Sea.

The Fleet at Constantinople, Frank Mason.

Then came the Ottoman armistice, and the Navy immediately took the opportunity to assert its new rights over the ancient Turkish capital. *Caesar*, with her four 12-inch guns and a crew of more than 600, more than twenty years old though she was, took the leading role in the procession across the Aegean to point her guns with due solemnity across the walls and monuments of the old city.

The *Goeben*, a newly built dreadnought-type battle cruiser, made the sweetest of prizes for the Royal Navy. At the beginning of the war she had outfoxed the British Mediterranean fleet, had bombarded the French ports in Algeria and then, with a series of ruses and stratagems, eluded the British ships as they chased her right across the Mediterranean until she made it to a safe haven beyond the Dardanelles. Then, handed over ostensibly to Turkey and renamed the *Yavuz Sultan Selim*, she had re-emerged to harass the British landings in Gallipoli, survive an encounter with the British battleship *Queen Elizabeth*, and escape back through the Bosphorus.

Earlier in 1918, she had ventured out again to surprise and sink two large British monitor gunships, and even menace the British fleet headquarters at Mudros. As it happened, she struck some mines, but once again contrived to get back through the Bosphorus. There was acute satisfaction among British sailors when the ship of which they had heard so much, and seen so little, was surrendered as a consequence of the Mudros armistice.

When HMS *Superb* and HMS *Lord Nelson* berthed in the port of Constantinople itself, amidst sailing ships, tugboats and ferries, it was decided that a show of military magnificence should be bestowed on the local population. And so the Seaforth Highlanders, in full ceremonial kilted kit, were disembarked to parade along the quay and into the city in a most emphatic demonstration of where power now lay.

Connard, who came from Southport in Lancashire, had actually volunteered, though nearly forty years old, and served with the Royal Field Artillery in France. He reached the rank of captain, but was eventually discharged from the Army with serious shellshock before finding himself appointed as an official artist with the Navy.

John Lavery spoke admiringly of Connard's courage in his new role 'taking on submarine work and frequently going into action'.

'It made me feel', said Lavery 'like those patriots who sit at home dauntlessly courageous in the face of the other fellow's danger.'

Connard was one of the handful of artists who had seen the reality of life aboard a warship. Another was Jan Gordon, who left an authentic picture of the care of wounded at sea.

Chapter Thirteen

Action at Sea

This is Gordon's account of the scene aboard a light cruiser after she had been in action:

The operating room was the stoker's bathroom, about twelve feet square. The centre of the room was occupied by a light portable operating table. The bathroom had a tiled floor and the blood could run away. Bare-armed, the fleet surgeon and a young doctor were working with desperate but methodical haste. They were just taking a man's leg off above the knee.

Our doctors were hard at it for eleven hours.

Aft, in the wardroom, as it was the largest room in the ship, we placed all the seriously wounded. The long table was covered with men, all lying very still and silently white.

An operating theatre at sea, Jan Gordon.

A young doctor was bending over one man. He signalled the sick berth attendant to remove him. Four stokers, still grimy from the stoke hold, lifted the body and carried it out. Two men were on the sideboard. Others were in armchairs. Water was slopping in from a hole in the side. In this ankle-deep flood, bloodstained bandages floated to and fro. One poor fellow lay like a marble statue on the wardroom table. There were no injuries on him. He was dying of shock. I used to go in and look at him. He seemed so peaceful and still that it was almost impossible to believe that in that body life was yielding inch by inch to death.

Chapter Fourteen

The German Navy Surrenders

The picture could not be more arrogant, decisive, final. HMS *Cardiff* steams imperiously across the canvas, white ensign and Union Jack flying. Astern of her, grey, cowed, submissively in line, trail the capital ships of the German High Seas fleet. Surrendered.

It is 21 November 1918, only ten days after the Armistice, 70 miles out from the Scottish coast in the North Sea, with only the brush of Charles Dixon to record this climactic moment for the Royal Navy – and the British Empire.

The deliberate attempt by the Germans to match and surpass the might of the Royal Navy had been one of the long narratives which had led up to, and helped to precipitate the Great War. Now that gargantuan investment of imperial German industry, invention – and blood – had been defeated. The humiliation had begun. It was less than two weeks since the guns had fallen silent on the Western Front and the German representatives had been herded into Marshal Foch's railway carriage in the forest of Compiègne.

The *Cardiff* had been sent to meet the High Seas Fleet as it set out to its final destiny. The German ships were required to appear at a point 56° west in the North Sea. The British Admiral Beatty had demanded the delivery of twenty-six battleships and cruisers and fifty destroyers.

As Dixon's painting shows, *Cardiff* encountered the German fleet and turned to lead it to the end of its war. On either side of the seventy-six German ships the British Grand Fleet, armed and ready for any signs of resistance, created a 6-mile wide corridor. But the doleful cortège showed no inclination but to steam steadily into capture and confinement at the Royal Navy base at Rosyth.

John Lavery had already been appointed an official artist with the Royal Navy, and he was summoned to record Admiral Beatty taking the formal submission of the German fleet aboard the battleship *Queen Elizabeth*. He recalled a cold and foggy morning – 'The German delegates were due to arrive at 11 am, but owing to the fog, mutiny and coal shortage, the surrendered fleet did not reach anchorage until 4 pm.'

He saw their arrival on the quarter deck and then witnessed the scene as the German Admiral Meurer was brought before the seated British officers: 'He spoke perfect English, his demeanour was dignified, but one could tell by his voice the strain under which he was labouring.' Lavery thought Admiral Beatty was 'somewhat severe on the fallen foe', but the German submarine commander was 'aggressive, if not defiant when he spoke'. At the end of hours of detailed instructions to the Germans, Lavery recalled that the British Admiral Tyrwhitt sighed and said to him, 'Actually, I am damned sorry for those fellows.'

HMS Cardiff leading the German fleet, Charles Dixon.

Beatty dictates to the German officers, Sir John Lavery.

The German Fleet at Anchor off Inchkeith, Charles Pears.

Within a few days of the meeting, the German fleet, quickly stripped of all but essential crew, was escorted again out from under the walls of Edinburgh and up to Scapa Flow in the Orkney Islands to await a decision on its final fate from the delegates at the Versailles conference.

Charles Dixon was already in his forties when he produced this picture. He had already established his reputation as a marine painter, having produced the iconic picture of Queen Victoria's Diamond Jubilee review of the Fleet at Spithead more than twenty years earlier. When war came, he was quickly engaged in painting some of the early encounters at sea, working from the descriptions of participants, including the action of the *Alcantara*, a British liner which had been converted into an armed merchant cruiser. She was patrolling north of Shetland, protecting the route to Russia, when she encountered what purported to be a Norwegian merchant ship. In fact she was a disguised German raider, the *Greif*.

Dixon's picture depicted the fierce fire-fight which then ensued, with both ships taking serious hits. Indeed, both went down, with the loss of nearly three hundred men, though as many were rescued after the timely arrival of a British destroyer and light cruiser.

But the most abject picture of submission by the German Navy had come only nine days after the Armistice. On 20 November, at dawn, there appeared over the horizon off the English coast at Harwich, twenty U-boats flying the white ensign of the Royal Navy. Twenty miles out from Harwich they had been boarded by British crews, who then brought them into harbour. The next day, another nineteen U-boats arrived and were subjected to the same ritual. Then the next day, another twenty, until by the end of the month there were 114 moored in the Essex harbour. The scene was the greatest assertion of Germany's final defeat.

One of the Harwich submarines was U60, painted late in the war by Claus Bergen off Heligoland, the great fortified German naval base at the mouth of the Baltic. U60 had had as deadly a career as any U-boat. With a crew of more than thirty, and equipped with half a dozen torpedoes, she made ten voyages to the Atlantic sea lanes and sank 52 ships, among them the *Armadale*, which was carrying British troops and their equipment to the Salonika front. After the surrender, U60 was listed to be scrapped, but actually sank off the English east coast on her way to the scrapyard.

Claus Bergen was already a well known marine painter when the war broke out, and was quickly appointed an official artist for the Kaiser. He was intrepid enough to actually join a submarine, the U53, and her captain Hans Rose, on an active mission in the Atlantic. By the outbreak of the Second World War he had become anointed by the Nazis as an approved painter, and actually sold ten of his pictures to Adolf Hitler.

Winston Churchill famously said that Admiral Jellicoe was the only man on either side who could win or lose the Great War in one day. The German U-boats were the weapon which, arguably, had nearly won the war on their own – and then lost it.

They and their intrepid commanders had been given free rein at the beginning of February 1917 to attack any shipping, British or not, which was carrying supplies to the Allies. This

U-boat off Heligoland, Claus Bergen.

unleashed the U-boats to attack even American ships in United States coastal waters. The Kaiser and his naval commanders believed that they could bring Britain to its knees before America could possibly enter the war and get significant numbers of troops across the Atlantic. The U-boats had already shown that they could range and operate over immensely longer stretches of ocean than even their own leaders had imagined. The Royal Navy was ill prepared for the disasters to come.

In the remaining months of 1917 the U-boats sank more than 2,500 ships. By the end of the war, that total had exceeded 5,500 ships sunk, more than 12 million tons of shipping in total. Belatedly, and probably only just in time, the Royal Navy reverted to the traditional convoy system, and managed to cut losses by half, though more than 1,000 ships still were lost in the last year of the war.

But the convoys were sufficient to keep Britain from being totally starved of food and war materials, and, more importantly, to allow the United States to build up Pershing's army in Europe to the point where it could play a crucial part in the final campaigns from Ludendorff's August 'black day' to the last victories in November.

Chapter Fifteen

Scapa Flow

William Lionel Wyllie's picture, The German Fleet Caged at Scapa Flow, records the scene before the sudden and final destruction of the German battle fleet and the Royal Navy's last lethal encounter in the aftermath of the Great War.

After the imperious demonstration of defeat imposed on the German Navy as it was hustled into the Firth of Forth to lie beneath the walls of Scotland's capital, the decision was taken to dispatch the 76 German ships, in batches, up to the Royal Navy's most northerly base at Scapa Flow in Orkney. The great ships were thus at least out of sight, if not out of mind, for the men fencing over their fate at the peace conference in Paris.

The German sailors were slowly released and sent back home in the early months of 1919, leaving just enough officers and men to maintain the ships' seaworthiness. All the victorious powers had their eyes on taking over all or part of the world's most modern navy. Japan made overtures to take possession of all the ships, including the U-boats which had slunk into Harwich. The French, the Americans, the Italians, all coveted some or all of the battleships. Meanwhile, they were in British hands, and as far away as possible.

Eventually the Allies drew up, and published, a deadline for decision – 15 June 1919. But the German commander at Scapa Flow, Admiral Ludwig von Reuter, through all these months of waiting, had secretly evolved a plan to foil all the aspirations of the victors.

On 21 June the British fleet put to sea on one of the frequent exercises they had been conducting over the past year to maintain their fighting efficiency. As they disappeared past the islands of Hoy and Ronaldsay and out to the open ocean, Von Reuter saw his opportunity and gave the coded order for all the German ships to be scuttled – 'Paragraph Eleven Confirm'. During the weeks of surreptitious preparation, watertight doors had been welded open, sea cocks made ready. Within minutes, watchers on the shore realized something was happening.

Edward Hugh Markham David was an eighteen-year-old sub lieutenant aboard the battleship HMS *Revenge* out at sea when the first messages arrived shortly after midday. The British fleet immediately turned and at full speed made for Scapa. David wrote:

> The sight that met our gaze as we rounded the island of Flotta was absolutely indescribable. A good half of the German fleet had already disappeared. The water was one mass of wreckage of every description, boats, carley floats, chairs, tables and human beings, and the *Bayern*, the largest German battleship, her bow reared vertically out of the

German fleet caged at Scapa Flow, William Lionel Wyllie.

Dawn at Scapa Flow, 1918, Sir Muirhead Bone.

Dawn at Scapa · Nov. 1918 · British Patrol meeting a German Battle Cruiser · Drawn by Muirhead Bone on the spot.

water, was in the act of crashing finally bottomwards, which she did a few seconds later in a cloud of smoke, bursting her boilers as she went.

Revenge's captain immediately ordered his officers to get the ship's boats launched to try and see if any of the German ships could still be saved. David's boat made for the battleship *Baden*:

We got alongside *Baden* which was going down fast and hurried below to see what we could do to save her. We closed watertight doors which kept her up temporarily.

We found one little German sub lieutenant, who was dragged up onto the upper deck. The flag captain told him he would be shot at sunset if he did not immediately take us below and show us how to shut off the valves. The German said he didn't mind if he was shot straight away.

Indeed the terrible part of the whole show was that the Huns hadn't got a weapon between them, and yet it was our bounden duty to fire on them to get them back to close their valves. It was quite obvious that the Huns would die to a man rather than save their ships.

The Royal Navy team did, in fact, manage to keep the *Baden* afloat long enough to be towed to the shore. Another 20 ships were successfully beached. But 52 ships went to the bottom. The German sailors took their small boats to escape the sinking ships, and a number were indeed shot as British sailors tried to force them to go back and save the ships. In one of the small boats the Royal Navy found Admiral von Reuter himself. He was taken aboard HMS *Revenge* to meet the British Admiral Fremantle. Sub Lieutenant Hugh David was present and recorded the scene:

As the German climbed wearily over the side there was a deadly hush on board. At first there was a pause, the German standing at the salute.

Fremantle:	I presume you have come to surrender.
Von Reuter:	I am come to surrender my men and myself [with a sweeping gesture towards the fast sinking ships] I have nothing else. I take upon myself the whole responsibility of this. It is nothing to do with my officers and men. They were acting under my orders.
Fremantle:	I suppose you realise that by this act of treachery, by this act of base treachery, you are no longer an interned enemy but my prisoner of war, and as such will be treated.
Von Reuter:	I understand perfectly.
Fremantle:	I suggest you remain on the upper deck until I can dispose of you.
Von Reuter:	May my Flag Lieutenant accompany me?
Fremantle:	Yes I grant you that.

German ships sinking at Scapa Flow, Bernard Gribble.

Bernard Gribble's painting is an eyewitness depiction of the events at Scapa, for he was actually in Orkney when the ships went down. He had been the first appointed official artist of the Great War, and because of his existing reputation as a marine artist, most of his work was with the Royal Navy. His painting of the German fleet being surrendered was actually bought by the future President Franklin Roosevelt and was to hang prominently in the Oval Office during his presidency. Coming from an artistic English family – his father was the architect of the Brompton Oratory in London – Gribble enjoyed a bevy of distinguished patrons, including King George V and Queen Mary, the Kaiser before the war, and later, the Onassis family.

In the post-war years many of the 52 sunken ships were successfully salvaged by an enterprising engineer, Ernest Cox. But there are still seven under the waters of Scapa, inspected these days only by scuba divers. The scuttling at Scapa was at one and the same time an embarrassment to the Royal Navy and a quietly successful solution to the debates about the German Fleet's fate. At least the ships would not fall into in anyone else's hands.

Chapter Sixteen

The American Experience

From the moment the Americans entered the war in April 1917 there had been official artists attached to their Army, and there was plentiful coverage back home in words and pictures in the newspapers and magazines of the time. But because of the distances involved, there had been very little home leave for American troops, and the direct impact of events 3,000 miles away was thus less intense.

It was only after the Armistice that returned American soldiers seemed able to distil the events they had seen and experienced into effective pictures, and it was more than two years after the peace that the extraordinary work of Claggett Wilson started to emerge. Wilson had gone to France as a private soldier with the first Americans in June 1917. He had been wounded and gassed at the Bois de Belleau engagement, lying for a day in brushwood until he was rescued. By the end of the war, now a lieutenant, he was an aide to General Nivelle. He recalled that as the American troops, after the Armistice, reached the little town of Niederbieber, he felt able to buy some materials and start work on the drawings which were to become the unique and utterly striking paintings shown in 1920.

It could be argued that beyond any of the other painters of the Great War Claggett Wilson succeeded in capturing the experience of fighting and living in the trenches of the Western Front. Raid on Our Trench and Dance of Death are pictures which are still a terror to contemplate. His visionary paintings like Vision on Easter Morning and Saviours of France reflect the intensity which produced stories like that of the Angels of Mons which recurred throughout the war. His Underground Dressing Station is truly sacramental in its ambition. Wilson recalled one of the situations he later painted:

Our headquarters were in an old farm near Villiers Cotterets, only a short and uncertain distance from the advancing Germans; word came we were to make a quick change to a position some miles to the north. Our only transport was a strange lot of horses, gathered oddly here and there. Shells had been falling in the rear, and there were frequent outbursts of machine gun fire from the neighbouring woods. I got on one of the horses (I later discovered he had been captured only the previous day). He pointed his nozzle toward the German lines and made straight for them like a bat back to hell. I turned him about a dozen times and as often he reversed himself and galloped off madly in the direction of the Hindenburg Line.

Raid on our Trench, Claggett Wilson.

Dance of Death, Claggett Wilson.

Saviours of France, Claggett Wilson.

The End of the War, Horace Pippin.

Eventually, Wilson abandoned his steed and survived. He was to live on, paint other wars and be recommended for a Nobel Prize.

For the New York African-American painter Horace Pippin, it was more than a decade before his great work The End of the War, emerged. Pippin had joined up in 1917 and went to France as part of the 369th infantry, the 'Harlem Hellraisers'. He had previously been working in an iron foundry, in a coal yard and selling second hand clothes. Of France he said, 'I did not care where I went. I asked God to help me and he did. That is the way I came through that hellish place. The whole battlefield was hell. No place for any human being to be.'

A German sniper eventually shot Pippin through the right arm and he was invalided home. His right arm seemed useless, but slowly, using his left arm to support it and trying painting as part of his rehabilitation, he regained some activity in and control of the limb. But it was 1930 before The End of the War appeared.

Despite the warplanes circling in the sky and the sinister tree crowns on the horizon, it is perhaps the most joyous picture of battlefield elation ever to have come out of the war. And the decade or more of memory and reflection before Pippin bestowed it on the public may only have refined his recollection of how it felt that day in November 1918.

Canadian War Memorial cartoon, Augustus John.

Chapter Seventeen

The Canadians

Augustus John was recruited by the Canadians as an official war artist. His The Canadians Opposite Lens, commissioned for a special place in the Canadian War memorial in Toronto, was what he called 'a vast cartoon'. He began it when he got home after the end of the fighting. The 'cartoon' was taken to Canada, but more than forty years later John had no idea what had happened to it – 'Not a single brick has been laid of this building, nor, I was told ever will be.'

But as can be seen, when it did eventually emerge it carried the enormous weight of distilled experience and emotion which Augustus John accumulated during the months he was living behind the lines in France in 1918. He first went to the Canadian sector near Arras. At this time there was a lull in hostilities:

> We were treated only to intermittent shell fire, aerial bombing, and occasional gas operations … Lievin was a completely devastated town opposite Lens, then in the occupation of the enemy. A few battered churches stood up among the general ruin. I found a battery which had been constructed within the ruins of a medieval castle. By getting friendly with the officer in command, I frequented it while making studies for the composition I had in view. From time to time a shell came over and, bursting, threw up its cloud of debris. When they came too near, our imperturbable major, ordering his men to take cover, sat with them, deep in the perusal of the *Daily Mail*, which I noticed he held upside down: there was an ammunition dump a few yards away.

At the time John was billeted in a large house in Aubigny, where he had a room he could use as a studio 'to draw and paint my soldiers'. It was there that he accumulated the array of paintings and drawings which eventually, as the end of the war came, he took back to England to use in the great mural commission.

Chapter Eighteen

Versailles

Georges Clemenceau was determined not only that the peace conference following the Armistice should take place in France, but that it should have a setting that would declaim the power and the grandeur of French victory. Hence the Palace of Versailles was chosen. Here was all the supreme architectural pomp of France's most illustrious King, Louis XIV. Even more important, the defeated Germans could be hauled into the famous Hall of Mirrors, where the Kaiser had had himself proclaimed Emperor after the German occupation of Paris in 1871. Indeed, Clemenceau was even able to contrive that the formal opening of the 1919 peace conference took place on the same date, 18 January, as the Kaiser's coronation forty-eight years earlier.

The Hall of Mirrors was built by Louis XIV's first minister, Jean Baptiste Colbert, who managed to seduce a number of Venetian glass workers to come to Versailles, despite the threats of death with which Venice, in those days, still managed to preserve her secrets of glass making and her monopoly of the trade.

Colbert nationalized the Gobelin family tapestry business in order to produce the adornments for the Hall of Mirrors, and kept meticulous accounts of all the silver decoration which glitters in the mirrors. As Orpen's pictures reflect, this was perhaps the most magnificent auditorium in Europe in which to host a discussion of great matters. Indeed, there was much to be done. Not only was the fate of Germany to be decided, along with the weighty matter of reparations, but also how to deal with the matter of the Russians, the fate of the Ottoman Empire and German possessions in Africa, China, even islands in the Pacific. William Orpen, appointed an official artist to the peace conference, was to listen to the intense debates on the new borders in Europe, on the fate of Germany's forces and particularly its navy, which at the time lay at anchor under guard in Orkney – a debate which was to be concluded decisively by the actions of Admiral Reuter.

John Lavery described Orpen's two depictions of The Signing of the Peace Treaty in the Hall of Mirrors at Versailles, as 'masterpieces'. They were, he said, 'the most powerful historical documents of the age and at the same time great works of art'.

Orpen left a vivid description of the day of the signing. He detested the battalions of bureaucrats in their black frock coats – 'the frocks', as he called them. He had trouble from them on the day in getting to his reserved seat in a window. But he made it just in time:

Clemenceau rose and said a few words expressing a desire that the Germans would come forward and sign. Even while he was saying these few words the whole hall was

The Signing of Peace in the Hall of Mirrors, Versailles, Sir William Orpen.

Signing Peace in Versailles, Sir William Orpen.

in movement – nothing but little black figures rushing about. Then amidst a mass of secretaries from the French Foreign Office, the two Germans, Hermann Muller and Doctor Bell, came nervously forward, signed, and were led back to their places. Some guns went off on the terrace – the windows rattled. Everyone looked rather nervous for a moment, and the show was over, except for the signatures of the Allies. These were written without any dignity. People talked and cracked jokes to each other across tables. Lloyd George found a friend on his way up to sign his name, and, as he had a story to tell him, the whole show was held up for a bit. All the frocks did all their tricks to perfection. President Wilson showed his back teeth, Lloyd George waved his Asquithian mane, Clemenceau whirled his grey gloved hands about like windmills, Lansing drew his pictures and Mr Balfour slept. It was all over.

Much of Orpen's disdain for the frocks comes through in his picture. He was shocked to discover that the Allied generals and commanders were taking little or no part in the peace conference – 'The Army was forgotten. Some dead and forgotten, others maimed and forgotten, others alive and well, but equally forgotten.' His fulminations emerge with full intensity in his notes of that Peace Treaty night:

Lord Derby gave a dinner for the Generals in their honour that evening, but I am certain the frocks did nothing. After all, why should they fuss themselves? The fighting was over. The Army was nothing, harmless. Why should they trouble about these men? Why upset themselves and their pleasures by remembering the little upturned hands on the duckboards, or the bodies lying in the water in the shell holes, or the hell and bloody damnation of the four years and odd months of war, or the men and their commanders who pulled them through from a bloodier and worse damnation and set them up to dictate a peace for the world?

Chapter Nineteen

General Smuts

Orpen's respect for the soldiers comes through in his picture of the South African General Jan Smuts:

> General Smuts sat, a strong personality with great love for his own country, and a fearless blue eye. I would not like to be up against him, yet in certain ways he was a dreamer and poet. He loved the people and hated the 'frocks'. He and I had a great night out once at the servants dance down in the ballroom of the Majestic Hotel. I found him down there during the evening and he said, 'You've got sense, Orpen. There is life down here, but upstairs it's just death.'

Smuts was, in fact, an almost unique figure at Versailles. There was perhaps no one else there who had actually fought in a war, then negotiated a peace treaty to conclude it and then become a key figure in the next war. Smuts had led Afrikaner troops in the Boer War, less than twenty years before. He had personally met Lord Kitchener to discuss a ceasefire and then led the discussions which led to the creation of the new Union of South Africa. Lloyd George had co-opted him on to the Imperial War Council during the war and then ensured that he came to Versailles with the Empire delegation. But when the Versailles terms emerged, Smuts was determinedly opposed to them. He said, 'I am grieved beyond words that such should be the result of our statesmanship' and described the requirement to occupy the Rhineland and hand over some German territory to Poland as 'full of menace for the future of Europe'. He thought the reparation demands were impossible.

Frances Stevenson, Lloyd George's secretary, mistress and later second wife, recorded that Lloyd George had great respect for Smuts, proposing at one point that he should take command of the Allied forces in Palestine, taking him to Rapallo to talk with the Italians at a key point in 1917 and even involving him in trying to solve the Irish problem. Consequently, the British Prime Minister, when he called a meeting of the Empire delegation to discuss objections to the peace terms, was most disturbed by the vehemence of Smuts views.

Though this meeting provoked another fortnight of discussions with the other Allies, the Versailles terms were little changed. In the end Smuts signed the Versailles treaty and went home to become Prime Minister of South Africa. He was to live to see his forebodings realized – and later to sign the treaty which ended the Second World War.

Jan Smuts, Sir William Orpen.

Chapter Twenty

Versailles Personalities

In contrast to Orpen, Augustus John, who had been recruited by Lord Beaverbrook as Canada's official artist, was airily dismissive of the Versailles scene – 'When I attended the Conference I realised that for me it held no pictorial possibilities. The aspect of the immense hall with its interminable rows of seated figures was visually merely boring.' Even the final act could not detain him – 'I wasn't going to wait for the signing of the Peace Treaty.' He took himself off to London.

But throughout the previous months of negotiations John had immersed himself with unashamed enthusiasm in the glittering social scene which flourished around the conference. Lord Beaverbrook would invite the young swells from the delegations to drinks and then usher them into a large dining room where every other chair was vacant – only to be quickly filled by a bevy of appealing young ladies whom His Lordship had recruited for his guests' entertainment. John records that Orpen left early, for 'such are the chains of mistress or wife'.

John himself became fascinated by the Arab delegation led by T. E. Lawrence and Emir Feisal. He painted them both a number of times, along with the great Arabian traveller Gertrude Bell:

> The Emir gave a luncheon party which I attended. I never ate so well: ah, those Arabian sweetmeats! Behind the Prince stood a gigantic Negro with a sword. This man, once a slave, had been liberated by Feisal. He would have died for his master, Lawrence told me.

The year after the War, John had an exhibition in London. Lawrence went, with his friend Lionel Curtis and later wrote to John: 'We were admiring me, and a person with a military moustache joined us and blurted out, "Looks a bloody sort of creature doesn't he?" Curtis, with some verve, said, "Yes". I looked very pink.'

Versailles proved very difficult for Feisal, Lawrence and the Arabs. The French tried to prevent them even landing in France, and only once did Feisal, resplendently dressed and wearing a gold scimitar, get to address the conference, with Lawrence translating. Lawrence, to his disgust, found that all the promises he had been making to Feisal and the Arabs about British support for Arab independence were worthless. The Sykes-Picot agreement, which had carved up the Middle East between France and Britain, prevailed. Feisal ended up installed as King of Syria in Damascus, but with French troops controlling the country. Within a year he was ousted and dispatched into exile.

Lawrence of Arabia, Augustus John.

Prince Feisal I, Augustus John.

Lawrence, with *Seven Pillars of Wisdom* still to be published, was taken up by the American journalist Lowell Thomas and turned into one of the first true international celebrities of the twentieth century, before joining the RAF as an anonymous airman and dying in a motorcycle crash.

Augustus John had the good fortune to meet a London friend in Paris, José Gandarillas, who let him have a studio adjoining his apartment on the Avenue Montaigne. Every night the apartment was thronged, and a band played music on the landing. 'Le tout Paris était là', as John put it.

Although John painted the Australian Prime Minister Hughes, the Belgian delegate Hymans and the Maharajah of Bikaner, 'a superb specimen of Indian manhood', and arranged to paint the South African General Botha 'who unfortunately suddenly died', his main artistic endeavours during the conference seem to have been focused on the ladies.

The former British Prime Minister Herbert Asquith's daughter Elizabeth was induced to pose – 'This brilliant young woman used to beguile the tedium of sitting by composing poetry which from time to time she recited aloud.' He was never short of female subjects. At a 'thé dansant' on the Champs Élysée given by the Duchess of Gramont, 'a new arrival arrested my attention. Even the Duchess, whose natural beauty was unassailable, looked, by comparison, somewhat rustic.' This turned out to be the Marchesa Casati, the wife of an Italian delegate, and 'it wasn't long before I added her to my list of sitters.'

The distaff side of the Peace Conference continued to prevail in his portraits: 'If the Duchess of Gramont failed me, there was always Miska, her friendly Scandinavian maid; if Louisa Casati was engaged, Louise Lorraine would perhaps be free.'

Towards the end of the war, John had, in fact, seen something of the battle zones. In uniform and with the rank of major although, as he reminded his correspondents, retaining his beard and thus the distinction of being the only such hirsute figure in the Army other than the King, he toured around behind the lines in Flanders in a chauffeur-driven car and painted a number of soldiers and wartime scenes.

But when the Allied attacks were being planned in the summer of 1918, John found his car and driver commandeered. He therefore returned to London and started work on the 'cartoon' intended for the Toronto War Memorial.

Opposite: *Australian Prime Minister Hughes*, Augustus John and overleaf (page 100) *The Marchesa Casati*, Augustus John and (page 101) *Elizabeth Asquith*, Augustus John.

Chapter Twenty-One

Woodrow Wilson

Woodrow Wilson had been re-elected President in 1916 on a firm 'No War' ticket. But within months his pledges were torpedoed by the German U-boats starting to sink US merchant shipping off the American coast.

Then came the Zimmerman Letter. This was a coded cable intercepted by British intelligence and deciphered thanks to the capture of a copy of the code 2,000 miles away in Mesopotamia. The letter from the German Foreign Secretary to his man in Mexico City offered the Mexicans substantial funds and supplies to help them invade and recapture Texas and New Mexico, if the United States came into the war on the Allied side. This proposal was less bizarre than it might seem, for the Americans had themselves already made incursions into Mexico the previous year in pursuit of Pancho Villa.

Wilson, who saw himself throughout his life as a peacemaker, had at first thought the Zimmerman cable was a forgery. But within a few weeks Zimmerman himself admitted it was genuine. The letter, together with the U-boat attacks, caused a furore across the United States, and Wilson was compelled to ask Congress to take the USA into the war on the Allied side.

But even as the American troops were landing in France, Wilson remained focused on trying to achieve a ceasefire. Early in 1918, he made a speech to Congress setting out his Fourteen Points which the United States would regard as a basis for peace. These included a return to many of the pre-war borders, freedom of the seas and the establishment of Wilson's grandest project, a League of Nations.

Though the Fourteen Points were raised in peace feelers by France and Italy, and even by the Ottomans, they had to wait for the Armistice talks with the Germans in Compiègne before they had any effect. There they provided part of the agenda for the Allies' demands.

As soon as the Armistice was signed, Wilson made it clear he was determined to take ship and attend the full peace conference planned for Versailles. He was the first incumbent President to leave the United States.

William Orpen was the official artist assigned to paint Wilson at Versailles. He was given a time of 2.00 pm at the Hotel Astoria and recalled: 'When I got to the door I found a large strange man ordering all the English motors to go one hundred yards down the Rue Vernet. No British car was allowed to stop closer.' Orpen made his way to Wilson's room and found two large men sitting in the only two chairs:

Woodrow Wilson, Sir William Orpen.

They took no notice of me, and were quite silent, so I proceeded to get ready. Taking off my belt and tunic, I started to squeeze out colours, when suddenly in marched an enormous man. He looked all round the room and said in a deep voice, 'Is Sir William Orpen here?' He walked up to me and, towering over me, looked down, and said in grave doubt, 'Are you Sir William Orpen? Be pleased to dress yourself and proceed to the door and prepare to receive the President of the United States of America.'

Shortly afterwards the President arrived, smiling as usual. But he was a good sort and he laughed heartily when I told him the story of the detectives. He was very genial and sat well, but even then he was very nervous and twitchy. He told endless stories, mostly harmless, and some witty.

The main thing Orpen remembered about the President was that he had great admiration for Lord Robert Cecil. He only had the one sitting, and the resulting portrait is of a President perhaps rather withdrawn, even sceptical, as well he might have been after the endless stresses of the conference.

Woodrow Wilson was to go back to Washington to face numerous tribulations. His health collapsed in the autumn of 1919, and it was more than five months before he was able to really get back to Presidential business. He failed to get the Senate to approve American membership of the League of Nations – his prime project – and Congress also declined to support him in taking on the mandate for Armenia or sending a warship and American marines to Baku to protect the Christians and American citizens there.

At home there was extreme agitation – seen as genuine Bolshevism – in the West Virginia coalfields, with some towns taken over by armed men even toting machine guns. At the same time, the wartime ally Italy was desperate for coal from the US, but there was no agreement as to how to pay for it. Wilson's Presidency ended in doleful contemplation of how his life's work had been thwarted.

Robert Cecil, Sir William Orpen.

Chapter Twenty-Two

Lloyd George

Lord Robert Cecil had earned President Wilson's respect during the extraordinary two weeks in February 1919 when the League of Nations was effectively invented round a table in the Crillon Hotel in Paris. Cecil and General Smuts had been given the task by Lloyd George of representing the British Empire's interests in Woodrow Wilson's prime project during the peace process. Wilson thought the creation of the League should take precedence even over the German terms.

Smuts himself had become a devout believer in the possibility of nations constructing a system of international law and supervision which could end the era of national conflicts. In those two weeks Cecil and Smuts took the lead in creating the rules of membership, the secretariat and the statement of aims, which did indeed prove the foundation of the League. Though the League of Nations is now remembered chiefly for its failures in Ethiopia and China, and finally, its inability to prevent a second World War, its work – and its mistakes – still served as a foundation for the new United Nations of 1945.

Lloyd George's mistress and secretary, Frances Stevenson, was painted by Orpen during the peace conference. 'A charming little man', she recorded. She was as close as anyone to the intense emotions and arguments which engaged the three main leaders in their almost daily face-to-face meetings, but it was to be more than fifty years before the diary she kept emerged to illuminate those days when a new world order was shaped.

When she and Lloyd George first arrived in Paris, they were taken to the battlefield of the Chemin des Dames – 'The place is a desolation, simply a series of shell holes. How men could have lived in it passes the imagination.' She saw the grave of her brother Paul, killed early in the war. But almost immediately they were plunged into the work of the conference.

On the first day, Stevenson noted, Lloyd George had a set-to with Marshal Foch over whether the Germans should be allowed a standing conscript army. 'D', as Frances Stevenson called him in the diary, 'got his way, for he had talked the whole thing over with Clemenceau in the morning.' Lloyd George believed it would force every country in Europe to keep a similar large army. Stevenson wrote, 'He is taking the long view about the Peace and insists that it should be one that will not leave bitterness for years to come and probably lead to another war.' During one of the discussions about Polish demands, Lloyd George said, 'Supposing you were Germany, no food, no raw material, stripped of her colonies, stripped of Alsace Lorraine, stripped of a large portion of her coal and iron. It is just a bleeding torso of the Germany that was.'

The leaders were well informed about the state of Austria and Germany; Stevenson recorded General Smuts coming to breakfast after he got back from Vienna:

He gave a most eloquently depressing account of the conditions there. It is a world completely gone to pieces. There is no authority, no business. Every shop is closed. There is scarcely any food there and everyone is starving. Smuts' batman and a soldier were walking in the street when a child came up and asked for food. They gave him a biscuit. Instantly the two men were set upon by a swarm of children who seemed to come from nowhere.

A few days earlier, an American journalist named Millard had been their breakfast guest:

He says the conditions in Germany are terrible. The rations allowed for a whole day are not enough to make what we should consider a decent breakfast. They do not mind the armies of occupation. In fact they are glad to have them there to preserve order. They curse the Kaiser and will hear nothing against the Allies. They blame their own government which led them into this war. They describe themselves as 'a betrayed people'.

When the British Admiral Wemyss was dispatched to put pressure on the Germans over the peace terms, Lloyd George, according to Stevenson, told him to make them realize the pistol he was holding to their heads 'was stuffed with sausages and not with bullets'.

Stevenson recorded in her diary the turbulent relations between Lloyd George, Clemenceau and Woodrow Wilson. On 14 March she wrote:

President Wilson arrived, and D says he can think and talk of nothing else but his League of Nations. I do not think they will ever get a move on until President Wilson has been put in his place, and D is the only person who can do it. Clemenceau cannot tolerate him at any price. If it were not for D, things would be impossible. [Later the same day] The French are still haggling about the right bank of the Rhine. D said to Clemenceau, 'You speak as though that would afford you security. Can you name a single river in this war that stopped an advance?' Clemenceau admitted he was right.

The next week, she recorded General Allenby coming to lunch:

A fine looking man, and one, I should imagine, who would stand no nonsense. D was urging him to give the French the facts about Syria, that the French would not be tolerated there. The French are very obstinate about Syria and are trying to take the line that the English want it for themselves and are stirring up the Arabs against the French. They are also making impossible demands about the indemnities, and on the whole are

Lloyd George at Versailles, Sir William Orpen.

behaving rather unreasonably. 'France is a poor winner,' said D. 'She does not take her victories well.' The real reason, I think, is that the French are terrified of a repetition of 1914. They cannot believe that Germany is defeated and feel that they cannot have enough guarantees for the future.

The three leaders, sometimes joined by Orlando of Italy, took into their own hands a formidable array of issues. Poland was ever-present, and Stevenson recorded, 'Paderewski came to lunch, with his story of Poland's woes.' She was instantly beguiled by him – 'There are very few people who have ever impressed me as much as he did. I could have listened to him for hours.'

And indeed she did. Paderewski gave them a panoramic exegesis of the origins of the Balkan peoples, from the Hittites to the Volgarians and the Armenians, who 'are the world's oldest race'. 'It just shows you,' said D, 'how difficult is our present task. We are digging up the foundations of a very old world.' Stevenson noted wearily:

> It is Poland at breakfast, lunch and dinner. D is dead against the 'corridor' system, under which a large slice of Germany containing 3 million Germans is lopped off and put under the Poles. D says it will simply mean another war. In the same way D is against the French retaining the left bank of the Rhine. He says the French are opening their mouths too wide.

Silesia, the military situation in Odessa, Yugoslavia, all were frequently on the agenda. Lloyd George talked to Foch, who constantly pressed to crush the Germans further, about Odessa, and they came to an agreement. Stevenson told her diary that a relieved Clemenceau said to Lloyd George, 'Mais vous êtes un grand general.'

The Italians, who had joined the Allies under the secret Treaty of London in 1915, were another problem. Orlando, their Prime Minister, was supposed to be part of the leaders' committee and was needed to sign off any agreements. But the refusal by the other three to give Italy Fiume, as well as trouble at home, led Orlando to flounce out and go back to Rome. Lloyd George dealt with this by summoning Imperiali, the Italian ambassador, and telling him that if the Italians were not back in Paris by Wednesday the Treaty of London would be null and void.

Stevenson records the scared look on Imperiali's face, for the Treaty had promised Italy chunks of the Tirol and Dalmatia – 'D repeated it. Imperiali hurried away.' Clemenceau did the same, and the Italians duly scampered back for the presentation of the peace terms to the Germans. The day was 7 May.

The four months at the beginning of 1919 had seen Clemenceau, Lloyd George, Woodrow Wilson – and, for some of the time, Orlando – closeted in intense daily discussion as they thrashed out the terms which were to be delivered to the Germans. The trouble was that the Germans, their army, their people and their new government, awaited the outcome of these discussions under the impression that the Armistice meant suing for peace, rather than an admission of defeat. Meanwhile, the Allies debated among themselves the terms which they, as victors, should impose on the vanquished enemy.

The new Socialist government in Weimar devoted huge bureaucratic resources in accumulating many volumes of documents with which they expected to confront the arguments and proposals of the Allies. Finally, the German delegation, led by the Prussian Foreign Minister Brockdorff-Rantzau, were summoned to Versailles. Having been given, as was now almost customary, a railway tour to Paris through the most devastated battlefields, they were then kept waiting in their hotel until the Allies agreed the last details of their terms.

Finally, Brockdorff-Rantzau was summoned. He refused to stand, and having seen the requirements of the Allies, sat and delivered what appeared to be a defiant speech. He then went back to his hotel.

The requirements of the Treaty which Brockdorff-Rantzau had to report back to the German government built on the terms of the Armistice to require the handing over of the Rhineland for at least fifteen years, the loss of 10 per cent of Germany's population, all her colonies in Africa and the Pacific, the abolition of her Air Force and the cashiering of all but 4,000 of her army officers. Above all, she was to pay reparations of $33bn.

The Germans were given a week to accept the terms. In the meantime, Marshal Foch lined up forty divisions to march into Germany if the Treaty was not accepted. The dismay in Germany caused many resignations from the government, and there were only hours to go when the Germans agreed that their new Foreign Minister Hermann Muller and a colleague, Johannes Bell, would come to Versailles to sign. Almost immediately, President Wilson took ship for home, as did Lloyd George.

The treaty witnessed by Orpen at his easel in the Hall of Mirrors was almost immediately denounced, not only by nationalists and revolutionaries in Germany but by the soldiers on the Allied side – most bitterly by Foch himself and the American General Pershing, who saw it as being merely a step towards another war with an undefeated Germany, but also by General Smuts and a number of civilian delegates, notably the Cambridge economist Maynard Keynes, who thought its terms could only lead to unrelenting hostility in Germany rather than secure a road to peace.

After the Hall of Mirrors ceremony, it took years and dozens of separate treaties to settle the fate of the new countries of Europe and the Middle East. And in the end the Germans only ever paid about half the reparations which they had agreed to, before Hitler and the new Germany renounced them entirely.

Frances Stevenson had recorded her impressions of the scene:

The Germans were very arrogant and insolent, and Brockdorff-Rantzau did not even stand up to make his speech. This infuriated the Allied delegates, and Hughes, the Australian Prime Minister, got up in a passion and came over to D and said, 'Is Clemenceau going to allow this fellow to go on like this?'

D said he felt he could get up and hit him. He says it has made him more angry than any incident of the war. If the Germans do not sign, he will have no mercy on them. He says, for the first time, he has felt the same hatred for them that the French feel.

I am rather glad that they have stirred him up, so that he may keep stern with them to the very end. If they had been submissive and cowed, he might have been sorry for them.

The actual signing of the Peace, six weeks later in the Palace of Versailles, Stevenson found 'rather disappointing'. She railed against the newspapermen, who seemed to take up half the room – 'The Press is destroying all romance, all solemnity, all majesty. They are as unscrupulous as they are vulgar.'

Although the Peace was signed, a huge number of issues remained for resolution. The Stevenson diary records, in February 1920, 'a furious D refuting French demands to take over the guardianship of the Holy Sepulchre in Jerusalem'. A few days later, she heard the Frenchman Millerand 'shouting and evidently protesting very strongly. The French are very much against any dealings with the Soviet Government.'

By the end of that month Lloyd George still found himself in all-day conferences on subjects ranging from reparations to the fate of German colonies. Millerand had replaced Clemenceau for France, and Nitti for Orlando and Italy – 'D shepherds them like a sheep dog. Millerand bolts off in one direction and Nitti in another. But D brings them back to the fold. It is what D excels in.'

Just seven months after the Versailles signing, Lloyd George was the only one of the quartet of leaders still in power. Clemenceau was defeated in an election, Woodrow Wilson was too ill to work and Orlando had been ousted in Italy. Stevenson called Lloyd George 'the Dictator of Europe', and he was to attend more than thirty further peace conferences before his own fall from power in 1922.

The Allied military leaders had been largely kept on the sidelines while the Council of Four worked on the document which was finally presented to the Germans on 7 May 1919. When they heard the terms which were to be imposed on the Germans, they were dismayed. Foch stood up and again repeated his demand that the border between France and Germany should be the Rhine. Otherwise, he said, in the next war Germany would simply bypass the French defences by going through the Ardennes.

General Pershing denounced the whole treaty. Smuts felt that the terms were so draconian that they would provoke resistance from the German people; the occupation of the Rhineland was especially 'full of menace for the future of Europe'. Pershing was to live to see his assessment of a twenty-year truce proved almost chronometrically accurate. Foch died before his predictions came true. Smuts lived to be sorrowfully vindicated.

Chapter Twenty-Three

The Treaty

The daily meetings of the three leaders in Paris had been the apex of a pyramid of furious and focused activity by officials and lobbyists in an array of committees.

The Arabs were led by the Emir Feisal with T. E. Lawrence. The Japanese were constantly concerned that their part in the Alliance should be sufficiently rewarded. A delegation of Koreans had literally walked most of the way to Paris

The document which emerged after scarcely four months to be presented to the new German government was unimaginably comprehensive. Where Woodrow Wilson's original peace proposals were composed of just fourteen points, the new treaty was set out in 440 articles. The first 26 of these defined how the new League of Nations would be constituted – and informed the Germans that they would be excluded from it. Then the draft dealt with the territorial losses which the Allies would inflict on the Germans:

Their colonies from Africa to the Pacific – German South West Africa to the Solomon Islands on the other side of the world – would be confiscated and ruled by Britain or her allies under what were called mandates.

On the border with France, Alsace Lorraine, seized by the Germans after the war of 1870, would be returned to the French.

The views of Lloyd George were overruled, and a corridor through German territory to the Baltic Sea was granted to the Poles, as well as the rich agricultural area around Posen.

The German port of Danzig was declared to be a free city and the League of Nations was to control it.

The Germans were told that in perpetuity they were not permitted keep any forces in the Rhineland; and the Saar coalfields were to be given to France – though only, oddly, for 15 years.

There were then detailed proposals, following up the terms of the November Armistice, setting strict limits on German armaments. The new Germany would be allowed no air force and no U-boats. The existing submarines had already been ordered to surrender in England, or were taken over in their home bases. The navy would be allowed six battleships and some smaller vessels.

The German army, which had exceeded two million during the war, would be reduced to a maximum of 100,000 men.

The treaty then went on to set out how Germany would be punished for starting the war and for the damage inflicted on her enemies:

The 'War Guilt' clause and its requirement of admission that Germany had started the War, though the least tangible of all the articles, was to cause the most persistent opposition to the Versailles treaty and become one of the planks of right wing and National Socialist agitation in Germany for two decades to come.

Germany was required to pay reparations for the damage suffered by the Allied nations in the four years of fighting. The amount was not immediately specified, but the Allied governments eventually assessed this as $33bn or 132bn gold marks.

Germany was forbidden to unite with Austria.

After the German delegation had appeared in the Hall of Mirrors and publicly signed the Treaty of Versailles, similar treaties were imposed on Germany's wartime allies:

Austria and Hungary were established as separate states. The Austrian Tyrol was handed over to Italy and the lands the Austro–Hungarian Empire had controlled in the Balkans were established as new independent states: Yugoslavia, Czechoslovakia, Rumania.

Austria, whose ships had been a serious threat to the Allies in the Mediterranean during the War, was allowed no navy at all. Her army could not exceed 30,000 men.

The Allies tried to exact reparations from both Austria and Hungary. But the two states were effectively bankrupt, had almost no resources, and could not pay.

Bulgaria, the first of Germany's allies to collapse, was told she could have no air force, a few torpedo boats, and no more than 20,000 troops. Reparations were set at more than 2bn francs, and as they still possessed an intact country after the war, the Bulgarians eventually managed to pay that bill.

Chapter Twenty-Four

The Cenotaph

The Cenotaph in London's Whitehall is now the most recognizable monument to the Great War in Britain. This is where the monarch or the Prince of Wales lays a wreath every year on Remembrance Day. An imposing structure in Portland stone, it was designed by Edwin Lutyens, who was seeking, he said, 'Simplicity and elegance and the lack of religious symbols and triumphalism'.

A Victory Parade took place in London scarcely two weeks after the Versailles Treaty was finally signed at the end of June 1919, although the construction past which 15,000 Allied soldiers and then hundreds of thousands of civilians marched on 19 July 1919 was a hastily conceived temporary fabrication of wood and plaster – Lutyens had only been officially commissioned when the Parade was planned. But it proved an enormously affecting focus for the emotions of the British people – the millions who made their way to London for that day and those who flooded into the cinemas to see the newsreels. Soon after, Lutyens was asked to transform it into the permanent monument which was installed on the site the following year.

The Victory Parade itself was the largest gathering ever seen in London. It had been organized in haste after it emerged that the French were going to have their own parade in Paris on 14 July. Lloyd George and Lord Curzon, who was chairing a peace celebrations committee, had initially planned a series of events in August. But evidently, they were concerned that the Paris parade might dilute the impact of gatherings a month or more later. So it was that troops from a dozen Allied armies gathered in Knightsbridge and Hyde Park, before marching through Whitehall and the Mall towards Buckingham Palace. Marshal Foch, the Allied Supreme Commander, was there, along with General John Pershing leading the American contingent and Field Marshal Douglas Haig at the head of the British troops.

Though it was, above all, a sacrament of victory, the King and the British Government were concerned that the dead and the maimed should have their part, so there were special stands near the Palace for the widowed and the wounded. The King himself took the salute beneath a golden cupola erected beneath the Queen Victoria memorial. King George V issued a statement on the day:

To the sick and wounded who cannot take part in the festival of victory, I send out greetings and bid them good cheer, assuring them that the wounds and scars, so honourable in themselves , inspire in the hearts of their fellow countrymen the warmest feelings of gratitude and respect.

London Cenotaph.

Chapter Twenty-Five

Étaples

The painter John Lavery did eventually get to France after the Armistice. His almost minimalist picture of the Étaples cemetery in Normandy is a reminder of the enormous task that faced the authorities in answering the demand for proper and dignified resting places for the dead. The British government would not permit relatives to recover bodies and bring them home. But mere wooden crosses and handwritten names would clearly not suffice to memorialize the fallen.

Étaples, already the biggest British cemetery in France, had been one of the most extensive training areas for British troops. It was here that the notorious Bull Ring was located, where men were pushed up to and beyond their limits by fanatical NCOs. Here the long-hushed-up Étaples mutiny took place in 1917, and there were sixteen hospitals, coping with more than 20,000 wounded, where, inevitably, many patients died.

By the time of Lavery's visit, nearly 11,000 soldiers were buried there. Already the authorities were planning to build three more imposing cemeteries – the first of what became a thousand in France alone. Étaples was to be designed by Sir Edwin Lutyens, who produced the enormously impressive memorial which to this day receives many thousands of visitors every year.

Lutyens had been recruited early in the war by the remarkable Fabian Ware of the Red Cross. Ware, collecting casualties behind the lines in France, had sought and received permission to record the names and locations of the myriad burial crosses scattered across the battlefields. He was acutely conscious of the need for relatives of the fallen to know where their sons and brothers lay. In past wars, the Army had tended to bury their dead in common graves with little or no ceremony. But Ware understood the strength of feeling back home, the certainty that the fatal letter from the Army could not just be the end of it, the palpable demand for some more enduring memorial. He became the founder of what is now the Commonwealth War Graves Commission.

In 1917, in a remarkable act of determination, and with the battle of Passchendaele barely concluded, Ware invited Lutyens and two colleagues to come with him to France. They stayed near the British Army headquarters at Montreuil. Lutyens, already a celebrated architect who had spent the last years before war broke out creating the new imperial capital of British India in New Delhi, seems to have immediately started to think how the new cemeteries could accommodate the different religions, backgrounds and ranks of the dead, and how the layout could be made imposing and yet welcoming to people who came to find their loved one's grave.

The Cemetery, Étaples, Sir John Lavery.

It was thus that the idea emerged of a single identical stone for every fallen man, rather than the cross that was normally used on the battlefields. Then Lutyens started to develop his idea for a large War Stone at the centre of the cemeteries, rather than a crucifix, or an altar. He wrote to his wife, the theosophist Emily Lytton, describing the graveyards as:

Haphazard from the needs of much to do and little time for thought. And then a ribbon of isolated graves like a Milky Way across miles of country where men were tucked in where they fell. Ribbons of little crosses each touching each across a cemetery set in a wilderness of annuals. For miles these graves occur from single pairs to close packed areas of thousands on every sort of site and in every sort of position, the bodies laid to face the enemy.

He described his idea to his friend J. M. Barrie, the author of *Peter Pan*:

It should be one great stone, 12 feet long set fair or finely wrought, without undue ornament and trickery or elaborate carvings, and inscribed thereon one thought in clear letters, so that all men may read and know the reason why these stones are so placed, facing the West and facing the men who lie looking ever eastwards towards the enemy.

Stone of Remembrance, designed by Sir Edwin Lutyens for the Commonwealth War Graves Commission.

Barrie warned Lutyens not to call the stone an altar. But he and Emily Lytton both felt the concept of the War Stone carried great power. When Lutyens then described it to Fabian Ware, he too embraced the idea. Wary though he was of creeds, Lutyens had an elevated concept of the divine in art and architecture which he intended to distil in his work on the cemeteries:

There is that in art which transcends all rules – it is the divine. With inspiration, rules are forgotten and some great immeasurable cycle of law is followed, unconsciously by some unaccounted impulse in my own kind of work. To short sight it is a miracle, to those a little longer sighted it is a Godhead. It is the point of view that ought to bring all arts into sympathy, and there is no ploy which cannot be lifted to the Divine level by its creation as an Art.

It is hard to visit his greatest work at Étaples and not encounter the resonance of these ideas.

Étaples Military Cemetery, France.

Chapter Twenty-Six

Lutyens

With the Armistice, there began the task of recovering the bodies of men who had fallen but not been removed to cemeteries. Ware's initiative had ensured that the location of many of the bodies was known, often marked with a rough wooden cross and the soldier's name, sometimes written in pencil.

A routine was quickly established. The bodies were dug up and wrapped in canvas to be taken to one of the locations which had been selected for a cemetery. Identification tags were checked and then, along with any personal effects, sent to relatives at home. This process went on until the formal end of the war in August 1921. By May 1920, 130,000 bodies had already been exhumed. From 1921 the new Imperial War Graves Commission took over the arrangements for dealing with bodies and for the design of cemeteries.

A headquarters was established in Longuenesse near St Omer, with six principal architects, including Lutyens and his old colleague and rival Herbert Baker, who favoured a style less classical than Lutyens and more reminiscent of an English village churchyard. Lutyens, who had sought the ideas of his friend, the celebrated garden designer Gertrude Jekyll, developed his vision of a 'green cathedral', with trees and hedges defining the cemetery space, along with his War Stone and a Cross of Sacrifice.

The architects sought assistance from the troops still in France. Wilfred van Berg described seeing a notice in his demobilization camp in France, asking for volunteers. 'Without a moment's hesitation I saddled my horse, galloped off to the neighbouring town, was interviewed and accepted.'

Though the basic principles of a plain headstone, a layout with bodies facing east towards the enemy, and the War Stone facing back towards them, were largely accepted, immense aesthetic effort went into making the cemeteries places of suitable solemnity and honour. Trees were carefully selected: hornbeams at Sanctuary Wood, alder at Choques, birches at Feuchy and limes at Serre Road, to suit both the new architecture and the soils of the region.

Rudyard Kipling, whose son John was killed in the war, guided the Commission towards the words which still resonate:

Their names liveth for evermore. A soldier known unto God.

The task of creating the cemeteries was to last until 1929, by which time nearly 1,000 – 967, to be exact – had been constructed in France and Belgium. Lutyens was responsible for more than a hundred of them.

Chapter Twenty-Seven

General Pershing

This smiling portrait of General John Pershing, the commander of the American Expeditionary Force, unashamedly reflects the consolation he found in Paris for the testing times he had endured right up to the Armistice and beyond.

Pershing had arrived in Paris in 1917 and endeared himself to the gathered crowds by proclaiming, 'Lafayette, we are here!', echoing the celebrated French Republican supporter of the United States in the War of Independence. The French government decided to commission the General's portrait and turned to a Romanian refugee artist, Micheline Resco.

She was to provide not only this enduring picture of the American hero but also the delights of her bedchamber to the General at a time when he had many stresses to confront. He would regularly have the American flag and his general's four stars removed from his Locomobile limousine staff car and be driven to meet her in the Rue des Renaudes. For almost thirty years they were to remain lovers, and they married when Pershing was close to death after the next war.

The Armistice infuriated Pershing. He had told the Allies, 'Germany's morale is low. Her allies have deserted her one by one. She can no longer hope to win. We should continue the offensive until we compel her unconditional surrender.' Pershing's views had found fervent support back home from former President Theodore Roosevelt and from Senate Republican leader Henry Cabot Lodge.

Pershing and Marshal Foch had had a stand-up shouting row, only weeks before, about the American role in an attack. Now, with the Germans seeking a ceasefire, Pershing told Foch that an armistice would lose the chance actually to secure peace on terms that would assure its permanence. When the terms were revealed, Pershing insisted that his troops keep moving forward throughout the hours up to 11.00 am.

Pershing was a general with extraordinary experience of war. Quite apart from his role in France, he had led a celebrated assault on an enemy hill in the Spanish-American war, served in the Philippines and commanded the campaign in Mexico to halt the adventures of Pancho Villa.

But, with the fighting stopped and the Versailles peace conference under way, the Generals found themselves excluded from the deliberations. When Pershing saw the final terms, he condemned them roundly with the words 'This is just a twenty-year ceasefire.' He was of course to be proved accurate to within a matter of months.

Micheline Resco
Paris 1921

Chapter Twenty-Eight

The Menin Gate

The Menin Gate, at Ypres in Belgium, remains the best known war memorial of all. Siegfried Sassoon, seeing it soon after its completion in 1928, denounced it as a loathsome reminder of a loathsome time. But the Austrian writer Stephan Zweig described it as:

Both spiritually and artistically profoundly impressive, erected by the English nation to its dead, a monument more moving than any other on English soil … This monument is to the six and fifty thousand English dead at Ypres whose graves could not be found, who

Opposite: *General Pershing*, Micheline Resco.
Above and overleaf: *The Menin Gate Memorial*.

lie somewhere crunched together in a common grave, mutilated beyond recognition by shells, or disintegrating in the water, to all those who have not their bright white polished stone, the individual mark of their last resting place. All these six and fifty thousand names are engraved in letters of gold – so many, so interminably many, that the writing becomes decorative. It is a memorial, then, offered not to victory, but to the dead without any distinction, to the fallen Australians, English, Hindus and Mohammedans, who are immortalised to the same degree, in the same stone, by virtue of the same death. In its really Roman simplicity this monument is more impressive than any triumphal arch or monument to victory that I have ever seen.

The Menin Gate is the work of Reginald Blomfield, one of the original architects recruited by the War Graves Commission. He went out to Ypres only a few months after the war's end, to seek in that landscape of devastation a suitable site for a memorial. Blomfield already had a vision of what he would like to create, inspired by a seventeenth century vaulted arch he had seen at Nancy, lit by openings in its crown and spanning the road. But he also sought a site with the utmost significance and so chose the Menin Road – 'It was through this opening in the ramparts of Ypres that our men went out to attack the German lines.'

The great lion on the top of the gate was made by Blomfield's friend, William Reid Dick – 'I told him I wanted a massive lion, not fierce and truculent, but patient and enduring, looking outward as a symbol of the latent strength and heroism of our race.'

It was to take Blomfield three years of sometimes cantankerous debate before he was finally able to realize his plans. And it was 1927 before the Gate was finished. Almost immediately, the Belgians instituted the nightly ceremony of sounding the Last Post, which endures so poignantly to this day.

And Blomfield was able to savour the approbation of *The Times*, which pronounced that the Gate 'has that austere beauty which befits the grand but cruel memories which it recalls'.

Chapter Twenty-Nine

The Unknown Warrior

William Orpen's painting of the flag-draped coffin of An Unknown Warrior depicts one of the most enduring symbols of the Great War.

This British memorial began with the utmost simplicity and ended in ceremonies which aroused profound emotions in the British people. It was an Army chaplain, David Railton, seeing a rough wooden cross on a battlefield in France with just the pencilled words 'An Unknown British Soldier', who conceived the idea of honouring the men with no known grave by burying one of their number, as he put it, 'amongst the kings'. His letter to the Dean of Westminster, passed on to Lloyd George, prompted the Government to ask Lord Curzon to recommend how it might be done.

Thus it was that the bodies of six soldiers from different battlefields in France were exhumed and taken to Arras to the chapel of St Pol-sur-Ternoise. Brigadier Wyatt of the War Graves Commission, accompanied by two other officers, came in, and Wyatt, closing his eyes, laid his hand on one of the coffins. This was to be the Unknown Warrior. The other five were taken away for a ceremony of reburial, and the coffin of the Warrior remained in the chapel. This was 7 November 1920.

The next day, the Warrior began a three-day journey which was planned in the smallest detail and attended almost every step of the way by respectful crowds. First he was taken to Boulogne's castle, where he was placed in an oak coffin made with timber from Hampton Court trees. A medieval sword from the Royal Collection was placed on his chest. The coffin was closed and bound with iron, and a shield was fixed on it bearing the words 'A British Warrior who fell in the Great War 1914–1918 for King and Country'.

Six black horses from the French Army then drew the coffin on a carriage through the streets of Boulogne, with French army buglers and hundreds of schoolchildren leading the cortège down to the harbour, where Marshal Foch awaited to deliver a farewell salute, before HMS *Verdun* and an escort of battleships carried the Warrior to Dover. From there the coffin was taken by train to Victoria Station in London.

The next day, the 11th, a horse-drawn gun carriage took the coffin through Hyde Park, down the Mall, past the new Cenotaph and on to Westminster Abbey, where it was buried in the nave. A guard of honour of a hundred holders of the Victoria Cross was in attendance, and the first of the many thousands who were to file past were women who had lost both their husbands and all their sons in the war.

Unknown British soldier, Sir William Orpen.

Despite all the crowds who were there that day, Orpen chose to paint the coffin in lone isolation in a marbled hall. The grave bears the inscription:

> Beneath this stone rests the body
> Of a British Warrior
> Unknown by name or rank
> Brought from France to lie among
> The most illustrious of the land
> And buried here on Armistice Day
> 11 November 1920 in the presence of
> His Majesty King George V,
> His Ministers of State,
> The Chiefs of his Forces
> And a Vast Concourse of the Nation.
> Thus are commemorated the many
> Multitudes who during the Great
> War of 1914–1918 gave the most that
> Man can give: Life itself
> For God,
> For King and Country,
> For loved ones home and Empire,
> For the sacred cause of Justice and
> The Freedom of the World.
>
> They buried him among the kings because he
> Had done good toward God and toward
> His House.

In France, on the same day, a similar ceremony took place, and there are Tombs of Unknown Warriors of the Great War in Canada, the United States, Australia, New Zealand and the other Allied nations.

To this day, the remains of British soldiers of the Great War are discovered during agricultural work or excavations. They are then given a full military burial in the nearest war cemetery. If they can be identified – and often three or four each year can be – their names are inscribed on tombstones and then removed from the list of still more than 50,000 names on the Menin Gate at Ypres 'for the fallen who have no known grave'.

Chapter Thirty

The Hall of Remembrance

By the end of the war, the official war artists' work had made a significant impact on the British public. There were the drawings and paintings in the newspapers and magazines, but also, in 1918, a number of exhibitions in London galleries, including one at the Leicester Gallery by the brothers Paul and John Nash.

Lord Beaverbrook, owner of the *Daily Express*, had been the initiator of the Canadian war artists scheme, which had recruited, among others, Alfred Munnings. By 1918 Beaverbrook had become Minister of Information in the British Government. He foresaw that one of the most effective ways of preserving a sense of the valour, purpose and sacrifice of the soldiers, sailors and airmen of the Empire, would be through the work of the war artists; and he therefore set in train plans for a great Hall of Remembrance to display their work. The project was to be on a grand scale and its architect, Charles Holden, envisaged a central pavilion in which there would be four vast 20ft paintings celebrating the comradeship of British and Imperial troops, with surrounding galleries and gardens.

Twenty painters were commissioned to produce work – and indeed did so – but it proved difficult to recruit the four main painters, though both William Orpen and Augustus John were approached. In the economic confusion of the post-war years, the Hall itself failed to materialize. However, the commissions for the Hall of Remembrance project did provide the stimulus for some of the most moving and memorable paintings of the Great War.

Paul Nash, who had served on the Western Front as an officer in the Artists Rifles, and his brother John, who had also been in the trenches, presented as their remembrance commissions two of the pictures which, a hundred years later, still epitomize the battlefields of France, The Menin Road and Oppy Wood. John Singer Sargent's picture Gassed became, perhaps the pre-eminent symbol of the fate of the fighting soldier.

Paths of Glory, Christopher R.W. Nevinson.

Harvest of Battle, Christopher R.W. Nevinson.

Oppy Wood, John Nash.

Chapter Thirty-One

The Art Establishment

The commissions for the Hall of Remembrance also marked a return of the British art establishment, members of which had been perhaps eclipsed by the young war painters; they also reflected a concern to show the colossal efforts made on the home front to ensure that the troops had the means of forcing victory.

A Two Year Old Steel Works, Charles Holmes.

An Advanced Dressing Station, Henry Tonks.

Divers at work repairing a torpedoed ship, John Wheatley.

A Two-Year-Old Steel Works by Charles John Holmes showed, in fact, the Steel, Peech & Tozer works in Yorkshire – a plant that survives to this day. Sir Charles, as he was properly titled, was an Old Etonian who had been Slade Professor of Fine Art at the University of Oxford, Director of the National Portrait Gallery and then Director of the National Gallery. He had become a noted portrayer of industrial landscapes and a frequent contributor to the Venice Biennale.

Alongside him was Professor Henry Tonks, formerly an autocratic teacher at the Slade School in London, who painted An Advanced Dressing Station in France. Many of the war painters, from the Nash brothers to Stanley Spencer, had experienced – and flourished under – his uncompromising views.

The Hall committee had prescribed that the commissions should include 'the war at sea and in the air', and as a result John Laviers Wheatley completed Divers at Work Repairing a Torpedoed Ship. Wheatley, another Slade graduate who had served in France with the Artists Rifles, was specifically commissioned to produce pictures of the Royal Navy. He went to Southampton and the headquarters of the Salvage Service, whose work he recorded in this picture – one of more than forty he painted in only a few months at the port.

Chapter Thirty-Two

War in the Air

The Remembrance Committee's aspiration to reflect the war in the air presented special difficulties. The pilots of the Great War were already glamorous figures: von Richthofen's Flying Circus were famous in Britain and France as well as Germany, and the Allies boasted air aces like Albert Ball, Mick Mannock and Billy Bishop.

Their exploits were viewed with admiration and wonderment from the trenches below, and the newspapers carried frequent descriptions of their victories. But the actual experience of flying in combat was rarely described or depicted by writers, poets or artists in those days of war. It was only years later that many of the first-hand accounts emerged.

Arthur Gould Lee, then a young lieutenant who had transferred from the Sherwood Foresters to the Royal Flying Corps and who was to end his career as an Air Vice Marshal, wrote the most vivid letters to his young wife Gwyneth Ann. In September 1917 his letter began:

We bagged four Huns today. Naturally we are slightly brimming over. It was a very similar patrol to yesterday afternoon. Four Pups at 12000 , with four Bristols at 8000. We went out at 9.30 and within half an hour found a two seater Albatross at 6000 which Nobby, Charles and I attacked in a steep dive on converging lines, as I forgot all about guarding tails. The observer stopped firing and collapsed. The machine at once went down in a dive over the vertical.

We climbed up and half an hour later engaged five Albatroses on our level. Exactly like yesterday I met trouble straight away as two got behind me and I couldn't shake them off. The other Pups were also fully engaged. I was twisting and skidding violently, as my two took it in turns to fire at me. I saw them both, one a pale blue, the other green grey, in between bursts of rak-ak-ak and tracer flashing past my nose. For once, I really had the gust up. I couldn't think how I could get away from them. And I couldn't even get one burst at either of them. Evading fire from the green grey, I nearly collided with the blue one when I did a half roll and found him just beneath me going on the same course. I was upside down and could see right into his cockpit. For one petrifying second I thought the two machines would close into each other. The pilot was looking up – he wasn't wearing goggles. He had a small moustache like me. We were so close I could almost have reached down and shaken hands. Fatuous thing to flash into one's mind in a fight, but it did, and the mind works fast. Then he pushed his nose down violently and vanished. I am sure he had as big a shock as me. I levelled out sweating with sheer funk.

Siege of Kut-el-Amara seen from the air, Richard Carline.

The Gorge at Wadi Fara, Sydney Carline.

There were writers like Gould who could express the ecstasies of flight in prose, although little poetry of the air has survived from that time, with the notable exception of W. B. Yeats' An Irish Airman Foresees His Death:

> I know that I shall meet my fate
> Somewhere among the clouds above;
> Those that I fight I do not hate,
> Those that I guard I do not love.

There were, however, two remarkable painters, the brothers Sydney and Richard Carline, who were to meet the aerial aspirations of the Hall of Remembrance committee.

Both brothers had been pilots in the war, and Sydney was shot down over the Somme in 1916 but survived. Both ended the war flying in the Italian campaign against the Austrians. Piloting Sopwith Camels, they managed to produce drawings and sketches which were later turned into paintings. Indeed, Sydney managed to establish a little studio in Vicenza to work in between his flying duties.

It was only after the fighting finished that the new Royal Air Force turned to them to depict the experience of combat flying and dispatched them together to the Middle East just six weeks after the Armistice. The Allied troops and air forces were still based across Palestine and Mesopotamia and, despite the capitulation of the Turks, there were still some operations going on against remnants of resistance, including by the Kurds.

The brothers went to Mosul, where the Royal Air Force were planning to bomb the Kurdish rebels, attached themselves to the Australian Flying Corps and were soon flying themselves, as observers, over the terrain where the campaigns of 1917 and 1918 had been fought. The result was a series of paintings which give the then unprecedented perspective of aerial views of ground action. The crucial destruction of a Turkish transport in the gorge of Wadi Fara was one of Sydney's key paintings, along with depictions of flying over Kirkuk and the desert at sunset.

The brothers then moved to Baghdad, before being recalled to the UK and preparing for what became an enormously successful exhibition in 1920 at the Groupil Gallery in London, where they showed more than three hundred drawings and paintings.

The Hall of Remembrance pictures, in the end, were consigned to the care of the new Imperial War Museum.

Chapter Thirty-Three

The Nash Brothers

For Paul Nash, the Armistice was to present him with the opportunity to turn his work in France into the large and ambitious paintings which he had yearned to complete.

Nash had volunteered as a private soldier in the Artists Rifles within days of war being declared and was soon in France. He had then been commissioned into the Hampshire Regiment and saw further service on the Western Front, before being gazetted as an official artist. Newly married in August 1914, he had sent sheafs of drawings back to his wife Margaret, along with the most vivid letters. Writing from behind the lines in May 1917, he told her that he had many drawings which he would soon be ready to send:

The little river which bubbles along through the town is a jolly bustling fellow, singing through the meadows, round the corners, like a swallow, head over heels through the mill, and on again past the alders. The whole country, the quiet of it, the sweet springtime, have all combined to make us sad and sick with longing for the end of this awful unending madness. One's mind widens out here alarmingly. I confess to you that this thing that brings men to fight and suffer together, no matter from what original motives, is a healthy force. The cause of the war was probably quite futile and mean, but the effect of it is huge. No terrors will ever frighten me into regret. What are the closing lines of Tennyson's Maud? 'I have felt I am one with my native land.' This is the emotion, and it is a satisfying one, to rest with when every other has turned bitter and dead.

Margaret had already organized two London exhibitions of her husband's war work. But now, with the guns silent, he set about completing the most implacable landscape painting of the war, The Menin Road. This was to be his principal commission from the Memorial Committee. The road itself ran from the small town of Menin to Ypres over a ridge, where there had been a prolonged fight over some German pillboxes. But the road carried the echoes of other fierce encounters and the names of well remembered battles – Sanctuary Wood, Hellfire Corner, Hooge Crater and Inverness Copse.

The picture is dauntingly large. Indeed, when Nash was completing it in a small studio in Gower Street in London in early 1919, legend has it that he had to climb out of the window to view it properly. With the shell holes and craters, the mutilated trees, the mud and the surviving little streams, The Menin Road encompasses, like no other work, the impact of the war on the landscape of the soldier's mind as well as on the earth itself.

The Menin Road, Paul Nash.

The end of the war, however, produced dilemma as well as fame for Nash. In his notes for an autobiography which he never completed, he wrote:

Struggles of a war artist without a war. Exhibition of war panels at Burlington House. Triumph of the Menin Road. I begin to design for the theatre. New life in a different world. New kinds of work. Wood engraving. Writing articles, designing textiles. Discovery of the Chilterns. I get up in the night and fall down. Black out.

Nash, in early 1918, had, by his own account, 'rescued' his younger brother John from the trenches. In fact, John had been appointed an official war artist. He had already served more than a year in the trenches and become a sergeant, taking part in the attacks at Passchendaele. He was one of only twelve survivors out of more than eighty men from the Artists Rifles who took part in an attack at Cambrai in the last month of 1917. John Nash was later to paint one of the most celebrated of the trench pictures, Over the Top.

After the Armistice he, too, was to remain afflicted by depression and memories of the war. He moved to the Buckinghamshire countryside and became a landscape painter. Many of his paintings, like The Cornfield or A Suffolk Landscape, reflect a healing bucolic peace. But it is impossible to look at The Moat at Kimble, painted in 1922, without seeing the visions and the nightmares of the war years conjuring themselves up in what is ostensibly a rustic English scene.

Previous page: The Moat at Kimble, John Nash.

Chapter Thirty-Four

Defeated Germany

For the German army, and then for the German people, 8 August 1918 was the start of the defeat of Imperial Germany, to be followed by the deterioration of the new republic into revolution, near-starvation and political chaos. In these last months of the war and the first years of the new republic, German artists created the most fearful and agonized images of their time.

Felix Kirchner painted himself with an amputated hand. He was to bring his own life to an end with a bullet in the head.

Otto Dix was already drawing the repellent images which would lead him into the post-war fury of his 1924 exhibition.

The 8 August offensive, principally by the British near Amiens, was prepared with the maximum amount of subterfuge; Allied planes prevented German aircraft from assessing what was going on in the build-up behind the lines. The attack seems indeed to have truly been a surprise, not only in its location and timing, but also in its tactics. Almost all movements in preparation were made at night. For the first time ever in war, the Allies managed to put an army of tanks – 456 of them, in fact – in the front line. Canadian and Australian troops, whose attacking qualities were much respected by the Germans, were used in feint attacks elsewhere in the line.

Then Providence, which had several times bestowed the concealment of a morning mist on German attacks, this time gave cover to the British.

There was even a place for the British cavalry. General Horne in his diary for that day in August wrote:

The First Cavalry Brigade got right on to Framerville and did great execution. I fetched up in Cayeux village. I saw a good many Boche dead. The prisoners came in in fifties and hundreds with just two of our men guarding them. They had no real heart. Some of our men told me they put up their hands at once.

In fact, German resistance remained stubborn in many parts of the line, and it took further pushes in September and early November, with American troops now leading the way in the east, before the emissaries were dispatched from Berlin to seek an armistice.

The defeated German soldiers found themselves straggling back after the Armistice to a country which was now desperately short of food, fuel and, indeed, law and order. Within

Self Portrait with severed hand, Ludwig Kirchner.

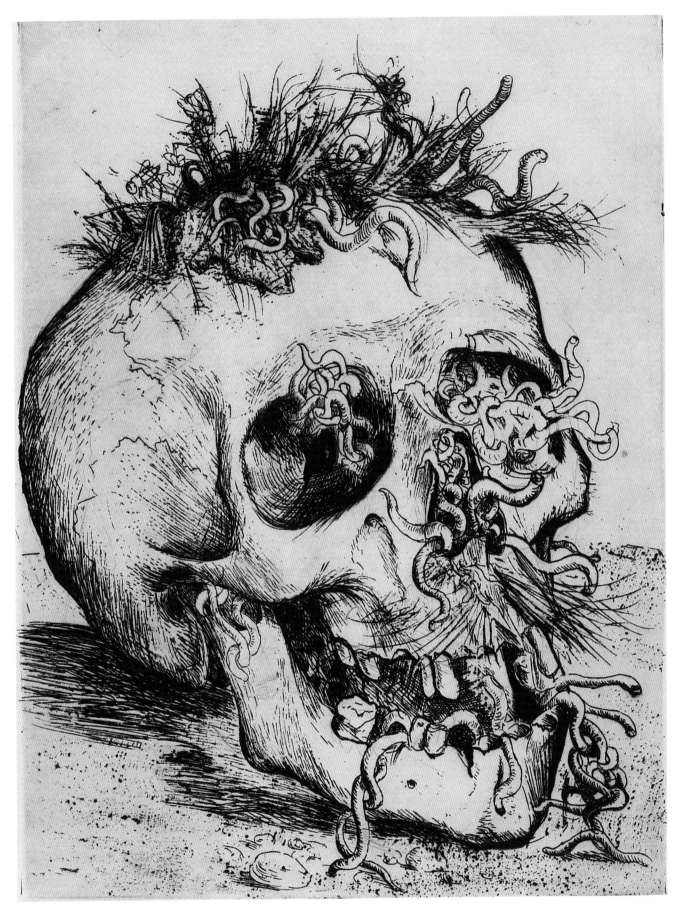

Skull, Otto Dix.

Soldiers Begging (Monument to Unknown Prostheses), Heinrich Hoerle.

War cripples, Otto Dix.

weeks the Spartacist rebellion broke out in Berlin: communists led by Rosa Luxemburg organized large-scale demonstrations, formed 'Soviets' and attempted to take over the government.

Ebert, Prime Minister of the new republic, retreated to Weimar. But he also encouraged the recruitment of a so-called Freikorps to take on the Spartacists. These were mainly ex-soldiers still in possession of their weapons and with access to motor vehicles and police information. Robert Graves' German cousin Conrad, with whom he had gone skiing only months before the war, survived the entire war in a Bavarian regiment, only to be shot dead by Bolsheviks months after the war's end, as his troop was trying to make requisitions in a village in northern Germany.

Within a few weeks the Spartacists were defeated and their leaders and many of their followers were murdered, but Ebert remained in Weimar. Meanwhile, Berlin witnessed desperate, maimed ex-soldiers begging in the street and rancorous complaints about how the Army had been betrayed – the 'stab-in-the-back' argument which was to have such powerful resonance for Hitler and the Nazis.

These became central themes for the radical artists, the Dadaists and New Objectivity group, who emerged from the war. Many were ex-soldiers themselves. Heinrich Hoerle produced his unrelenting Soldiers Begging within months of the war's end. He had been an Iron Cross-winner and artillery specialist on the Western Front, and his home town of Cologne had been overrun by the Allied armies. But it was not long after his return that he produced this painting, showing not only a strong sense of pacifism but anger and sympathy for the plight of the men who had come back to no jobs, no support and little hope.

At the same time, Otto Dix, whose drawings were to become emblematic of the pacifist reaction to the war and its end, was working on a large collection of drawings. War Cripples is as pointed as its title. Nearly 100,000 amputees had come home from the war, and Dix shows us the wheels, crutches and other contraptions which they used to get themselves about, with an ironic reference to the shop they are passing – a shoemaker's.

Dix had joined up eagerly at the beginning of the war and became a machine gunner. He was part of the phalanx of German gunners who mowed down the advancing British at the battle of the Somme, and he even started to train as a military pilot. But by the end of the war he had started to become the dedicated pacifist who exhibited in 1924 the array of dreadful paintings in his series Der Krieg – his skull with worms crawling out of the eye sockets and mouth, and his menacing Storm Troops Advancing under a Gas Attack.

Dix's fellow Expressionist Ernst Ludwig Kirchner, a noted painter of nudes and the human figure, had also been a volunteer in 1914, but shellshock forced him to leave the Army. His Self Portrait as a Soldier, showing his right hand amputated and his symbolic impotence, is a clear vision of self, for although his mind was shattered, he had not actually lost a hand.

George Grosz was one of the artists Dix met and befriended. Grosz's Pillars of Society continues the theme of furious rejection of the war and its consequences.

Stormtroopers advancing, Otto Dix.

Pillars of Society, George Grosz.

The Allies had kept up their blockade of German ports in order to maintain pressure on the German government to sign the Versailles treaty. In consequence, large parts of Germany were still desperately short of food. Early visitors, after the peace, found the country and towns largely undamaged, for the fighting had never reached them. But they were beset by children begging for food and reported that most people were existing on very crudely made bread, with meat and vegetables simply unobtainable. The plight of the children in particular very quickly caused both British and American Quakers to try to bring supplies and help to Germany. The future American President Herbert Hoover initiated what became a very large relief effort, under the name 'Child Feeding', which was to provide, in the end, for almost two million German children.

But then, when the Germans fell behind in their reparation payments, the French army marched into the Ruhr and took over the coal and steel workings which would have provided some basis for German economic recovery. Soon there was hyperinflation in Germany, eventually reaching many billions of marks to the dollar or pound.

Augustus John's painting of Gustav Stresemann portrays the man who, four years after the war, as Chancellor and then Foreign Minister of Germany, produced policies which allowed his country to start recovering from the war's worst economic effects. He introduced a new currency, the Rentenmark, secured on industrial assets, and started the process of rapprochement with France which was actually to see him nominated for a Nobel Prize. Augustus John had been in Berlin when, he recalled:

Stresemann was the leading statesman of the new German Republic. Our Ambassador, Lord D'Abernon, persuaded him to sit for me. I liked him well. Cast in no heroic mould, he presented none the less an interesting exterior. That square cranium housed a cultured mind, informed with the old German idealism. His portrait, when finished, was not in the least flattering, but Stresemann faced it bravely. His wife was taken aback, I could see. Frau Stresemann, a lively and accomplished Jewess, was always to the fore in the social life of Berlin.

Stresemann was involved in many attempts, such as the Dawes Plan and the Locarno treaty, to find a firm basis for Germany's status after the war. But shortly before his premature death he told a British diplomat:

If the Allies had obliged me just one single time, I would have brought the German people behind me. The minor concessions the Allies made always came too late. Thus nothing else remains for us but brutal force. The future lies in the hands of the new generation. The German youth, who we could have won for peace and reconstruction, we have lost. Herein lies my tragedy, and there the Allies 'crime'.

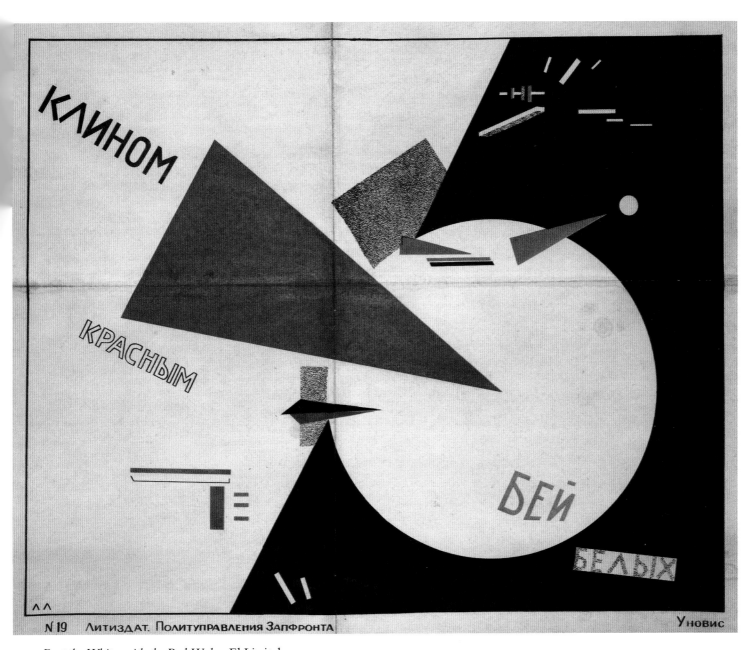

Beat the Whites with the Red Wedge, El Lissitzky.

Opposite: *Gustav Stresemann*, Augustus John.

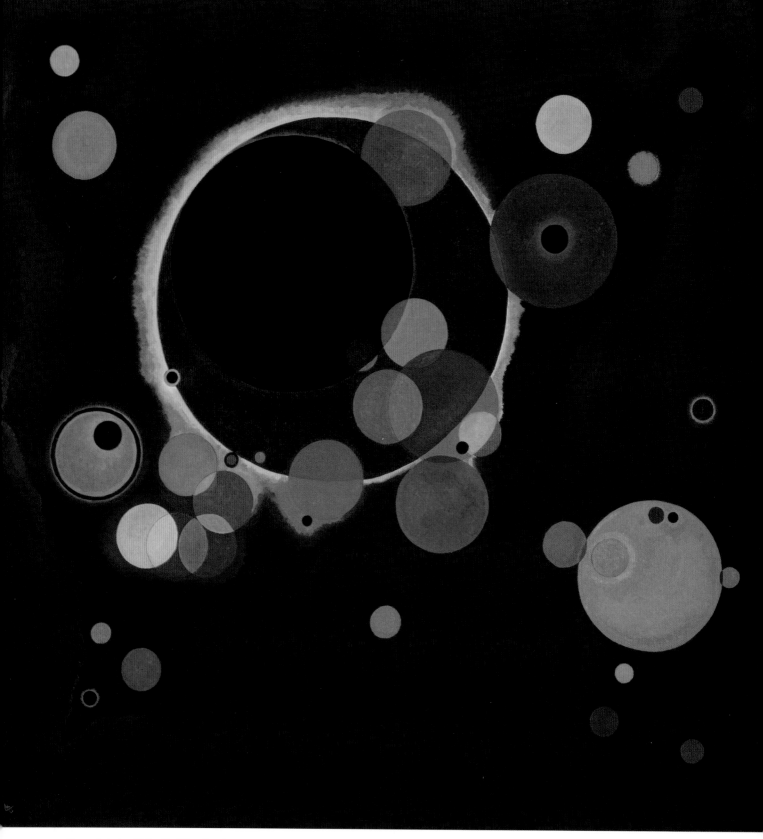

Several circles, Wassily Kandinsky.

In Russia, wracked by revolution, then a civil war, and then the beginnings of state terror, the artists were required to contribute to the proletarian struggle. Lissitsky with his painting Beat the Whites with the Red Wedge, was an early exponent of what was to become the classic form of Stalinist art, idolizing the workers, demonizing the capitalist enemies and defining the ambitions and achievements of the state.

In utter contrast, Kandinsky, deported as an alien from Germany, where he had been a notable member of the Blue Rider group, succeeded in clinging to his convictions, seeking always, as he proclaimed, 'the spiritual in art'. He contrived to return to Germany in 1921, having been invited to join the Bauhaus in Munich, thus escaping the official odium which was to engulf modernist artists in Russia in subsequent years.

Chapter Thirty-Five

War Memorials: Britain

Only twenty years earlier, the heroic feats – and defeats – of the Boer War had inspired the first wave of civic memorials across Britain. They display great detail, often naming battles and, as the York memorial does, listing separately those killed in action, those dying of wounds and those dying of disease.

Even before the Armistice was signed in 1918 there were already committees all over Britain raising money and contemplating the most appropriate way to remember the fallen and give bereaved families a focus for their grief. Indeed, in 1918 there were already memorials in a number of towns and villages: Eric Gill's Virgin and Child in Briantspuddle in Dorset, crucifixes in Hickleton and Royston in South Yorkshire, and others.

Above: *Newcastle 'Pals' Memorial*, Sir William Goscombe John.
Opposite: *Memorial to Machine Gun Corps*, Derwent Wood.

ERECTED TO
COMMEMORATE
THE GLORIOUS
HEROES
OF THE
MACHINE GUN
CORPS
WHO FELL IN
THE GREAT
WAR

Saul hath slain his thousands
but David his tens of thousands

MCMXIV

MCMXIX

Thousands of communities across Britain decided to use their memorial funds for practical purposes – the Memorial Halls, sports grounds and clubs and institutes which are still, a hundred years later, in everyday use.

But there were also, almost invariably, monuments naming the dead and often those who had served, erected in a public place around which memorial services could be held. Within the year – by November 1919 – Armistice Day had become the date selected for annual remembrance. These monuments were to become hugely ambitious in style and absorb the energies and talents of a great number of artists and sculptors. Indeed, for some years it could be said that creating war memorials was by far the most engaging artistic activity of the time.

There are many thousands of these Great War memorials, large and small, in almost every town and village, in the squares and churchyards, and besides the roads of Britain. More than a hundred sculptors are recorded as working in this unparalleled burst of activity. Many produced a number of works in those intense years straight after the war. Louis Roslyn created at least twenty-five monuments from Antrim in Ireland to Essex and Hampshire. There was pressure to work quickly, as communities longed to see how the funds they had raised were turned into monuments to the glorious dead or consolation for the bereaved.

Some, like The Response, Sir William Goscombe John's memorial to the Newcastle Commercial 'Pals', were hugely ambitious; it shows a mass of soldiers saying farewell to their womenfolk, and young boys dedicated to admiring and succeeding their elder brothers and fathers. A woman holds up her baby for a last kiss from the father. Another soldier, hugging his daughter, is urged to hurry on by his young son. There are civilians – men as well as women – who had taken part in the war effort, a comradely crowd which seems to reflect the ethos of the Pals battalions. Sited in gardens beside the Barras Bridge, The Response, draped in a huge Union Jack, was unveiled by the Prince of Wales, accompanied by Earl Haig, in 1923.

The Response was commissioned by the local MP, Sir George Renwick, a wealthy ship owner, who had been very active in supporting the raising of the Pals battalions in Newcastle. He made no secret of the fact that his funding of the monument was also in recognition of his own great good fortune, in that he had sent five sons to the war, all of whom had survived. One, John, famously took his pack of hounds with him to France. Another, Septimus, won the Military Cross.

Other monuments were bitterly controversial. Derwent Wood's magnificent David still stands resplendent at Hyde Park Corner in London. But this is a monument to the short-lived Machine Gun Corps, still carrying the defiant and much denounced inscription: 'Saul hath killed his thousands. But David his tens of thousands.'

Derwent Wood had already, in 1919, provoked a renewed outburst of feeling in Canada against the Germans, when the Canadian exhibition in London showed his bronze sculpture Golgotha, resurrecting the story of a Canadian sergeant who, it was said, had been crucified when he fell into German hands near Ypres. The sculpture is unflinchingly horrifying: the soldier, still in his greatcoat and uniform, his head hanging like so many depictions of Christ

Opposite: *Canada's Golgotha*, Derwent Wood.

Christ driving the moneychangers from the temple, Eric Gill.

Edward Horner Memorial, Mells.

on the cross, is pinned with bayonets through his hands to a barn door, while German soldiers watch in the background.

The exhibition was due to open just when the proceedings of the Peace Commission were beginning in Paris. There was an outburst of protest in Germany denying that any such incident had ever taken place, and the Canadian Prime Minister Robert Borden requested an investigation. The bronze was withdrawn and it was seventy years before even reproductions of Golgotha were permitted by the Canadian authorities. But there does seem to have been evidence that the atrocity had actually been committed. The Canadians had statements from at least two of their own soldiers – one of them, in fact, a Victoria Cross winner – that they had seen the body. The dead man was even named as Sergeant Brant. Then a note from a nurse, unearthed by documentary maker Iain Overton in 2002, added strong credence to the story, naming the victim as Sergeant Harry Band.

Derwent Wood was already Professor of Sculpture at the Royal College of Art when he started volunteering at Wandsworth Hospital in London, which specialized in treating facial wounds and where early plastic surgery was being attempted. The surgeons and staff knew that once physical recovery from facial injuries had been achieved, patients still dreaded the reactions which their disfigurement aroused.

Wood persuaded his colleagues to try a new approach. He took plasticine casts of the soldier's face. Then, in weeks of painstaking work, from photographs and from undamaged portions of the face, he created thin copper masks to restore the facial shape and appearance that the soldier had had before his wounds. These were then carefully painted in enamel to tone with the skin colours of the patient, and he was able to go about with, as the doctors reported, new self confidence. There were certainly several hundreds of these operations, before further advances in plastic surgery overtook the technique.

Another controversial sculpture was Eric Gill's memorial for the University of Leeds. It shows Jesus driving the money-changers out of the temple, with the clearest possible implication to that most mercantile of British cities that the money men had been a cause of war.

Many of the sculptors are forgotten, though their works endure and still serve their purpose, at least each November, a century after they were made. Some of the celebrated artists of the day, however, did become intensely involved in these projects.

Alfred Munnings, known at the time, and today, almost exclusively, for his paintings, was the inspired choice of Edward Lutyens to join him in creating a large sculpted memorial at Mells in Somerset to the Hussars Lieutenant Edward Horner, who had been killed in 1917. Munnings produced the half life-size horse, with Horner, bareheaded and calm, his cavalry sword and helmet hanging by his side. The statue, placed in the church of St Andrew, was one of the first of the major commissions for family memorials which were to occupy the devotion of many artists of renown.

At Trumpington in Cambridgeshire, the clean and spare style of Eric Gill gives a unique distinction to the relief memorial, with St George slaying the dragon while protecting a grateful maiden. Kathleen Scott, widow of Robert Falcon Scott of the Antarctic, was one of the rare women sculptors, producing at least three statues, including one at Slimbridge. Jacob Epstein, bitter opponent of the war as he was, proposed a work 'hundreds of feet high and set on some high place where all could see it and where it would give out its warning'.

For many of the sculptors, central themes were victory over evil, heroic endurance and devotion to comrades and duty. But there was a strong religious feel to many of the figures, with the promise of resurrection and heavenly reward. Indeed, it is the image of Christ on the Cross which is at the centre of hundreds of the war memorials, equating the sacrifice of the soldiers' lives with the story of Calvary. Others show soldiers at prayer or the Virgin Mary succouring the troops.

Gilbert Ledward was one of the artists invited to contribute to the Hall of Remembrance. He proposed a separate mausoleum with stone reliefs and sculptures illustrating the Stations of the Cross, starting with Jesus being condemned to death. Like the Hall, the Mausoleum was never built, though Ledward went on to create more than half a dozen memorials, more with themes of glory than of religious significance.

War Memorials: Australia

The monuments to the fallen appeared with astonishing speed. More than three hundred were already completed and dedicated by 1921. But new ones were being erected well into the 1930s. Their role endures, as the focus of not only the Great War but often all subsequent wars too.

In Australia, with more than 60,000 of their soldiers killed in Mesopotamia, Gallipoli and on the Western Front, there was tremendous public pressure to commemorate the war dead. This resulted in arguably the largest and most awe-inspiring Great War monument of them all, the Australian National War Memorial at Canberra, as well as the great Shrine of Remembrance in Melbourne. But these projects became embroiled in long and bitter, often political, controversy, and lack of funds in the Thirties recession also delayed their construction for decades. The National War Memorial was not opened until after another war had started, in 1941.

The idea for the National Memorial came from the historian Charles Bean, who had been in France during the battles of 1916. But it was nine years before a competition was organized to produce a design. The judges could not decide between the ideas of two architects, John Crust and Emil Sodersten, so they were encouraged to cooperate and produced the design which is now the most prominent building in Canberra, with its Hall of Memory, the Tomb of the Unknown Australian Soldier, its imposing approach and the engraved names of all the dead. Every evening now, except at Christmas, there is a Last Post ceremony: a piper and a bugler come down from the Hall of Memory, and the story of one of the names is read out.

The Melbourne Shrine of Remembrance encountered even more problems. When its design by local architects and war veterans Philip Hudson and James Wardrop was revealed in 1922, the local Murdoch newspaper denounced it as too severe, a 'tomb of gloom' in their words, and began a campaign to have the funds diverted to a hospital or homes for war widows – an echo of disagreements being aired in other countries across the world. In Melbourne it became a party political issue, with the Victoria Labour Party supporting the Murdoch view. When the National and Country Party came to power in Melbourne, they supported the building of the Shrine, and it was eventually completed and dedicated on Armistice Day 1934 by the Duke of Gloucester, with a crowd of more than 300,000 attending.

Stimulated perhaps by the furore over the Memorials, painters and artists in Australia continued to engage with the war to a much greater extent than their European colleagues.

The Menin Gate at Midnight, Will Longstaff.

Man in the Mud diorama, Peter Corlett.

Will Longstaff, a wounded Gallipoli veteran, produced his supremely evocative The Menin Gate at Midnight in 1927. It toured Australia in 1928 and 1929, invariably attracting large crowds.

Almost seventy years after the war, Peter Corlett was commissioned to produce his fibreglass diorama, Man in the Mud, which became one of the most appreciated artworks at the Memorial.

Chapter Thirty-Seven

Post-War Blues

As Paul Nash said, the immediate aftermath of the war came as a disturbing challenge to many of the war artists.

After their exuberant and celebratory pictures of the Armistice, the artists who were to become the adventurers of the new worlds of post-expressionist painting, soon found themselves living in a post-war world of almost anarchic disarray.

In Britain, the troops were impatiently waiting to be demobilized by a bureaucratic system which decreed an impenetrable system of priorities. Students and agricultural workers were at the top, and the old soldiers who had seen the whole war through were chagrined to discover they came after the new boys, who had scarcely been a year in uniform.

By 1919 the country already had more than a million unemployed, even before the tide of returning servicemen washed into the industrial towns. The influenza epidemic, unprecedentedly acute, was killing and incapacitating millions in Britain and beyond. There were military mutinies – not just the Navy at Spithead, but even the Guards. Robert Graves saw hundreds of them marching defiantly through Brighton. By 1921 official statistics reported 86 million man-days lost to strikes. The cost of living had gone up by 25 per cent.

Christopher Nevinson, creator of Paths of Glory and La Mitrailleuse, who found his picture, The Harvest of Battle, already in 1919 being denounced as 'too grim', took himself across to Paris and the artistic world he had known before and during the war. He encountered Picasso, moving on from Cubism, and Modigliani, whose work he bought. He wrote, 'Military conditions still existed at this time in Paris, all manner of regulations as to food and drink, the opening and closing of cafes.' But the mood in the art world was changing. Nevinson came back to London for an exhibition by the Imperial War Museum, only to find his previously celebrated pictures hung high and almost out of sight:

That for me was a day of disillusion. I did not conform to their idea of public opinion. I did not paint heroic pictures for the glorification of war. I had spent hours in the air, in the front line trenches, even in front of the front line trenches with the Lovat Scouts. And the sum of it all was that I was now informed that I was lacking in artistic integrity.

Assaulted by recurring depression – 'That finished me with the Imperial War Museum. I have never since had anything to do with it' – he threw a huge party, denounced the London art scene and took ship for New York on a liner crowded with returning Canadian troops, whom

Overleaf: *The Soul of the Soulless City*, Christopher R.W. Nevinson.

The Garden Enclosed, David Jones.

he described as spending their time doing nothing but gamble. But he soon came home, only to make a second visit later and find his paintings derided and ridiculed by American critics.

Nevinson lived to see another war and to chronicle his own bleak mood and the critics' accusations of his declining powers. Yet it is hard to look at The Soul of the Soulless City, or the mordant late work, The Twentieth Century, without feeling still the intense dark talent which emerged through and beyond the Great War.

Nevinson never painted another war picture after the war's end. But for some of the war artists, those years were to dominate the rest of their lives. For the painter and poet David Jones, twenty years were to pass before he felt able to publish his long narrative poem In Parenthesis, with its vision of abandoning his rifle as a tourist memento:

> Leave it under the oak
> Leave it for a Cook's tourist to the Devastated Areas and crawl
> As far as you can and wait for the bearers.

And it was six years after the war that Jones produced his painting, The Garden Enclosed. He explained: 'A trench lived in in 1915 might easily get into a picture of a back garden in 1925 and by one of those hidden processes transmogrify it – impart, somehow or other, a vitality which otherwise it might not possess.'

Jones's title for the picture comes from *The Song of Solomon*: 'A garden enclosed is my sister, my spouse, a spring shut up, a fountain sealed.'

Chapter Thirty-Eight

Stanley Spencer

Stanley Spencer, already a much lauded young artist before the outbreak of war, had quickly volunteered for the medical service and found himself first at a hospital in Bristol and then, from 1916, out in northern Greece where the British and French were confronting the Bulgarians, a largely inactive sector until the last few weeks of the war. It was in the October, after the Allies launched an attack, that Spencer found himself involved in hazardous situations as a message-carrier, getting perilously close to the front line and witnessing the officer for whom he was working fatally shot right beside him.

All of a sudden, the Bulgarians surrendered, and Spencer, who had been ill with malaria, was shepherded home via Italy and France to his village of Cookham in Berkshire. It was only then, with the war over, that he found himself appointed – and remunerated – as an official war artist. He wrote that throughout his time in Macedonia he had dreamed of finishing a painting, Swan Upping, which had been lying facing the wall in his family bedroom. His first act on coming home was to finish it.

But unlike many of the war artists, the aftermath of the war was to provide Spencer not with protracted agonizing about what to paint but with the opportunity to do his greatest work. It was suggested to him that he might make a very large painting for the proposed Hall of Remembrance, perhaps on the subject of a religious service at the Front. Neither the Hall nor the painting ever materialized.

However, throughout his time in Macedonia and on his return home Spencer had been drawing and thinking about the war and its effect on him. He later recalled a scene which had inspired one of his paintings:

I was standing a little away from the old Greek church which was used as a dressing station and operating theatre. Coming there were rows of travoys with wounded and limbers crammed full of wounded men. One would have thought that the scene was a sordid one, a terrible scene, but I felt there was a grandeur. All those wounded men were calm and at peace with everything. I felt there was a spiritual ascendancy over everything.

Back home at Cookham, Spencer created the first of his Resurrection pictures with the grave crosses thrust aside and the dead soldiers rising from their resting places. But he had also started to conceive and draw a narrative series reflecting his experiences in the war. By 1923 he was writing:

I have hardly been out at all. I have been so much moved by a scheme of war pictures that I have been making compositions for, that all my time here has been on this. I have drawn

a whole architectural scheme of the pictures. The end wall is to be a tall circular topped picture of the resurrection of the soldiers in Salonica. This idea is at present the vaguest, and yet I know it will be the best. On either side four pictures, quite small.

Spencer spent the summer showing his drawings to Augustus John and others, including T. E. Lawrence of Arabia – 'He liked very much my scheme of war pictures.' Then came the fateful and fortunate encounter which was to produce one of the most sublime and unique of all memorials of the war.

Spencer first met Mary Behrend and her husband Louis at one of Lady Ottoline Morrell's parties; they already owned Spencer's Swan Upping picture. Meeting them again at a friend's house in Dorset, Spencer showed them his drawings. They were both entranced, for they had been fretting for a long time over a memorial to Mary's brother Hal – Lieutenant Henry Willoughby Sandham – who had served in Macedonia at the same time as Spencer. He had come home in 1919 extremely sick and had died, effectively in Mary's arms, later that year.

The Behrends had bought some land from Lord Caernarvon at Burghclere, near Newbury in Berkshire, with the idea of building a chapel, but the project had not yet got off the ground. Within a few weeks in the summer of 1923, however, they had gained such confidence in Spencer's ideas that, by September, they told him they would commit to it.

It was to take more than a decade to bring it all to fruition. First the chapel had to be built. With Spencer insisting on the most rigorous measurements and design detail – one architect could not stand the interference and left – it took three years before the chapel itself was built. Only then could Spencer start to install his painting and work on the frescos which were to cover all the walls. For one period of three years Spencer and his wife Hilda lived in a cottage nearby and he worked in the chapel every day.

The Behrends financed Spencer throughout the decade it took to complete the chapel, and the finished work is extraordinary. The Resurrection, as Spencer had planned, is the overwhelming vision which visitors see as they enter. But around the walls is the narrative of the life of a Great War soldier of which Spencer had long dreamed. There is a convoy arriving, and a dugout, but also bed-making and sorting of laundry, as he had seen in his Bristol hospital, a wonderfully diaphanous Reveille, as the soldiers are summoned from sleep, tea-making and cases of frostbite.

It was to be the winter of 1932 before Spencer finally wrote to Mary Behrend to say that the work was accomplished and the Sandham Memorial chapel could, at last, be dedicated.

Opposite: Sandham Memorial Chapel, *Resurrection of the Soldiers*, and overleaf: *Ablutions, Kit Inspection* and *Reveille*, Sir Stanley Spencer.

Chapter Thirty-Nine

Women in War

Flora Lion's 1918 picture of women at the Phoenix Works in Bradford in Yorkshire, confident and comradely as they wait in the canteen queue, marks in retrospect the apogee of women's place in British society for a decade or more at least. The canteen itself was an innovation designed to serve women workers, but also an institution that survived in British industry.

Within a year there had been enacted a piece of legislation, the Restoration of Pre-war Practices Act, which obliged firms to offer returning men the jobs they had held before the war, and so to dispense with the women who had taken up their places in factories and other workplaces. More than three quarters of a million women were thus dispatched back to home and hearth, or to whatever employment they could find.

The number of women employed in the manufacture of munitions had quadrupled in the war years, and there was no dispute that they could do the job. As early as 1915, the British Association, meeting in Manchester, heard a Report on Women's Work which frankly concluded:

It may be safely said that women can successfully handle very much heavier pieces of metal than had previously been dreamed of. Moreover they have shown themselves capable of successfully carrying out arduous processes such as forging which have hitherto only been performed by men. In the making of fuses they excel, and have rendered great service in the delicate work involved in the manufacture of the wings of aeroplanes.

The women in Flora Lion's painting were a significant part of a force of more than 4,000 workers employed by the Phoenix Dynamo company. The firm still made dynamos, but as the war progressed it moved into munitions, manufacturing millions of shells. One of the Phoenix directors designed aircraft, and by 1917 they were also building seaplanes and flying boats for the Admiralty,

As the women in British factories were laid off after the war, there were some compensations. The vote came in 1919, though only for women aged over thirty. For those women still in work there was some move towards more equal pay. But even in jobs like selling train tickets or Post Office work, women in the mid-1920s were still earning barely half as much as men.

Flora Lion was a well known portrait painter. She had been commissioned late in the war to paint factory scenes in Leeds and Bradford, and along with two other women artists, asked to present pictures to the post war British War Memorials Committee, though in the end the committee was dissolved without taking any of their work. Flora Lion, in fact, went on to become a noted painter of the female members of the British Royal Family.

Women's canteen at the Phoenix Works, Flora Lion.

Statesmen of World War One, Sir James Guthrie.

Chapter Forty

The Wartime Leaders

The forces of South Africa had played a crucial role right from the beginning of the war, but only after the defeat at home of pro-German Boers who took up arms against the South African government and, for a time, seemed a serious threat. It was, in fact, the Boer War Afrikaner veterans, notably Louis Botha and Jan Smuts, who had made peace with the British scarcely twenty years earlier, who led the troops that crushed the rebellion. They then went on to defeat the German forces, first in South West Africa and then in East Africa.

With the crucial trade routes to the Indian Ocean thus safely protected, a large contingent of South African soldiers then sailed to fight on the Western Front and in Mesopotamia. And it was the South African Sir Abraham Bailey, diamond millionaire, friend of Cecil Rhodes and husband of the intrepid aviatrix Mary Bailey, who took it upon himself to commission the great valedictory painting of the Great War Statesmen of the Empire.

Few of the men who guided the British Empire and its Allies to victory and then, at Versailles, imposed the victors' terms, survived long in public office after their wartime task was done. In Sir James Guthrie's comprehensive picture, there are already the ghosts of the dead – Kitchener in the slightly ethereal background and Botha in his military uniform next to the Indian delegate to the Peace Conference, the Maharajah of Bikaner.

Lloyd George is there, of course, but within a year of the peace, he was the only one of the four leading statesmen still to be in active office. Clemenceau had lost an election, Orlando of Italy was ousted, Wilson was incapacitated by illness. Lloyd George, although he was to last until the autumn of 1922, experienced constant trouble in Ireland at the same time as trying to organize the Genoa conference, which he had proposed to try and settle the great economic issues bequeathed by the War. He said:

> If the European countries had gathered together the mobile wealth accumulated by centuries of industry and thrift on to one pyramid and then set fire to it, the result could hardly have been more complete. International trade has been disorganised through and through. The recognised medium of commerce, exchange based upon currency has become almost worthless and unworkable. Vast areas upon which Europe has hitherto depended for a large proportion of its food supplies and raw material have been completely destroyed for all purposes of commerce.

This was the last attempt by the last of the former leaders to deal with the consequences of the war. King George V did not like the idea of him going to Genoa, as Frances Stevenson recounted:

'I suppose you will be meeting Lenin and Trotsky', the King said.

Lloyd George responded, 'I am not able to choose the people I am forced to meet in your service. A little while ago I had to shake hands with Sami Bey, a ruffian who was missing for the whole of one day and was finally traced to a sodomy house in the East End.'

The French were also less than keen to have such a meeting. But it did take place, and it was agreed to try and restore the gold standard and provide at least a more solid base for rebuilding the shattered economies, particularly of Eastern Europe.

Lloyd George was never to hold office again. But Frances Stevenson noted that Winston Churchill, who is highlighted in Guthrie's picture, 'was still nursing his ambition'.

As well as half a dozen British politicians, from Asquith to Bonar Law, there are two Australian prime ministers in the painting, Joseph Cook and Billy Hughes. Hughes had been a vociferous force at the Peace Conference, demanding that Australia should receive its share of the reparations being extracted from the defeated powers. He was supported in this and in deleting the racial equality clauses of the Versailles treaty, which he thought threatened the White Australia policy, by the premier of New Zealand, William Ferguson Massey.

Canada's Robert Borden, Prime Minister of the senior British Dominion, had seen his country provide large numbers of troops for France throughout the war. More than 60,000 were killed, and in 1919 there were still Canadians, reluctantly dispatched by their own government, involved in the fighting in Murmansk and the north of Russia. Borden had been insistent that Canada should be involved in the decision making at Versailles. Thus the original British delegation to the Peace Conference was transformed into a British Empire delegation, with Borden a constant reminder to Lloyd George that the Dominions' interests should be heard. He saw the Versailles agreement through the Canadian parliament, then in 1920 he, too, retired from office.

Edward Morris had been Prime Minister of the independent Dominion of Newfoundland at the beginning of the war. An ardent imperialist, he had immediately called a large public meeting and set up the Patriotic Association of Newfoundland, which recruited and paid for the Newfoundland Regiment. Morris was co-opted by Lloyd George into the Imperial War Cabinet. He was in England when the Newfoundlanders suffered in one of the deadliest encounters of the war, attacking at Beaumont Hamel in 1916. More than 700 men went over the top and only 63 answered the roll call at the end of the day. At the end of 1917, when he was again in Europe, Morris simply sent a letter home resigning as Prime Minister. Lloyd George immediately ennobled him, and Baron Morris, as he became, only occasionally visited his homeland thereafter.

Statesmen of the Great War, set beneath the Winged Victory, was the third in a trilogy of large paintings – the other two are of naval and army commanders – which Abraham Bailey commissioned, with the idea that they should be shown round the Dominions and the Empire to demonstrate how effective the British Imperial lands had been in rallying to the cause of the Great War.

Appendix

The Armistice Terms

WESTERN FRONT

I.   Cessation of operations by land and in the air six hours after the signature of the armistice.

II.   Immediate evacuation of invaded countries – Belgium, France, Alsace-Lorraine, Luxembourg – so ordered as to be completed within fourteen days from the signature of the armistice.

German troops which have not left the above-mentioned territories within the period fixed will become prisoners of war.

Occupation by the Allied and United States forces jointly will keep pace with evacuation in these areas.

All movements of evacuation and occupation will be regulated in accordance with a Note [which was served on the German Commander-in-Chief.]

III.   Repatriation, beginning at once, to be completed within fourteen days of all inhabitants of the countries above enumerated (including hostages, persons under trial or convicted).

IV.   Surrender in good condition by the German armies of the following equipment:
        5,000 guns (2,500 heavy, 2,500 field)
        30,000 machine-guns
        3,000 *minenwerfer*
        2,000 aeroplanes (fighters, bombers – firstly D.7s and night-bombing machines)
The above to be delivered *in situ* to the Allied and United States troops in accordance with the detailed conditions laid down.

V.   Evacuation by the German armies of the countries on the left bank of the Rhine. These countries on the left bank of the Rhine shall be administered by the local authorities under the control of the Allied and United States Armies of Occupation.

The occupation of these territories will be carried out by Allied and United States garrisons holding the principal crossings of the Rhine (Mayence, Coblenz, Cologne), together with bridgeheads at these points of a 30-kilometre (18.63 miles) radius on the right bank, and by garrisons similarly holding the strategic points of the regions. A neutral zone to be set up on the right bank of the Rhine between the river and a line drawn 10 kilometres (6.21 miles) distant, starting from the Dutch frontier to the Swiss frontier. In the case of inhabitants, no person shall be prosecuted for having taken part in any military measures previous to the signing of the armistice. No measure of a general or official character shall be taken which would have, as a consequence, the depreciation of industrial establishments or a reduction of their personnel. Evacuation by the enemy of the Rhinelands shall be so ordered as to be completed within a further period of sixteen days – in all, thirty-one days after the signature of the armistice. All movements of evacuations and occupation will be regulated according to the Note.

VI.   In all territory evacuated by the enemy there shall be no evacuation of inhabitants; no damage or harm shall be done to the persons or property of the inhabitants. No destruction of any kind to be committed. Military establishments of all kinds shall be delivered intact, as well as military stores of food, munitions, equipment not removed during the period of evacuation. Stores of food of all kinds for the civil population, cattle, etc., shall be left *in situ*. Industrial establishments shall not be impaired in any way, and their personnel shall not be moved.

VII.   Roads and means of communication of every kind, railroads, waterways, main roads, bridges, telegraphs, telephones, shall be in no manner impaired. All civil and military personnel at present employed on them shall remain. Five thousand locomotives, 150,000 waggons, and 5,000 motor lorries, in good working order, with all necessary spare parts and fittings, shall be delivered to the Associated Powers within the period fixed for the evacuation of Belgium and Luxemburg. The railways of Alsace-Lorraine shall be handed over within the same period, together with all pre-war personnel and material. Further, material necessary for the working of railways in the country on the left bank of the Rhine shall be left *in situ*. All stores of coal and material for upkeep of permanent way, signals, and repair shops, shall be left *in situ,* and kept in an efficient state by Germany as far as the means of communication are concerned during the whole period of the armistice. All barges taken from the Allies shall be restored to them; the Note appended as Annexure 2 regulates the details of these measures.

VIII.   The German Command shall be responsible for revealing all mines or delay-action fuses disposed on territory evacuated by the German troops, and shall assist in their discovery and destruction. The German Command shall also reveal all destructive measures that may have been taken (such as poisoning or pollution of springs, wells, etc.), under penalty of reprisals.

IX.   The right of requisition shall be exercised by the Allied and United States Armies in all occupied territory, save for settlement of accounts with authorised persons. The upkeep of the troops of occupation in the Rhineland (excluding Alsace-Lorraine) shall be charged to the German Government.

X.   The immediate repatriation, without reciprocity, according to detailed conditions which shall be fixed, of all Allied and United States prisoners of war; the Allied Powers and the United States of America shall be able to dispose of these prisoners as they wish. However, the return of German prisoners of war interned in Holland and Switzerland shall continue as heretofore. The return of German prisoners of war shall be settled at peace preliminaries.

XI.   Sick and wounded who cannot be removed from evacuated territory will be cared for by German personnel, who will be left on the spot, with the medical material required.

EASTERN FRONTIERS OF GERMANY

XII.   All German troops at present in any territory which before the war belonged to Russia, Romania or Turkey shall withdraw within the frontiers of Germany as they existed on August 1st, 1914, and all German troops at present in territories which before the war formed part of Russia must likewise return to within the frontiers of Germany as above defined as soon as the Allies shall think the moment suitable, having regard to the internal situation of these territories.

XIII.   Evacuation by German troops to begin at once; and all German instructors, prisoners, and civilian as well as military agents now on the territory of Russia (as defined on August 1st, 1914) to be recalled.

XIV.   German troops to cease at once all requisitions and seizures, and any other undertaking with a view to obtaining supplies intended for Germany, in Romania and Russia, as defined on August 1st, 1914.

XV.   Abandonment of the treaties of Bukarest and Brest Litovsk and of the supplementary treaties.

XVI.   The Allies shall have free access to the territories evacuated by the Germans on their eastern frontier, either through Danzig or by the Vistula, in order to convey supplies to the territories or for the purpose of maintaining order.

EAST AFRICA

XVII.   Unconditional evacuation of all German forces operating in East Africa within one month.

GENERAL CLAUSES

XVIII.   Repatriation, without reciprocity, within a maximum period of one month, in accordance with detailed conditions hereafter to be fixed, of all civilians, interned or deported, who may be citizens of other Allied or Associated States than those mentioned in Clause III.

XIX.   With the reservation that any future claims and demand of the Allies and United States of America remain unaffected, the following financial conditions are required:- Reparation for damage done. While the armistice lasts no public securities shall be removed by the enemy which can serve as a pledge to the Allies for the recovery or reparation for war losses. Immediate restitution of the cash deposit in the National Bank of Belgium and, in general, immediate return of all documents, specie, stock, shares, paper money, together with plant for the issue thereof, touching public or private interests in the invaded countries. Restitution of the Russian and Romanian gold yielded to Germany or taken by that Power. This gold to be delivered in trust to the Allies until the signature of peace.

NAVAL CONDITIONS

XX.   Immediate cessation of all hostilities at sea, and definite information to be given as to the location and movements of all German ships. Notification to be given to neutrals that freedom of navigation in all territorial waters is given to the naval and mercantile marines of the Allied and Associated Powers, all questions of neutrality being waived.

XXI.   All naval and mercantile marine prisoners of war of the Allied and Associated Powers in German hands to be returned without reciprocity.

XXII.   Handing over to the Allies and the United States of all submarines (including all submarine cruisers and mine-layers) which are present at the moment with full complement in the ports specified by the Allies and the United States. Those that cannot put to sea to be deprived of crews and supplies, and shall remain under the supervision of the Allies and the United States. Submarines ready to put to sea shall be prepared to leave German ports immediately on receipt of wireless order to sail to the port of surrender, the remainder to follow as early as possible. The conditions of this article shall be carried out within fourteen days after the signing of the armistice.

XXIII.   The following German surface warships, which shall be designated by the Allies and the United States of America, shall forthwith be disarmed and thereafter interned in neutral ports, or, failing them, Allied ports, to be designated by the Allies and the United States of America, and placed under the surveillance of the Allies and the United States of America, only caretakers being left on board, namely:

      6 Battle-cruisers.
      10 Battleships.
      8 Light cruisers, including two mine-layers.
      50 Destroyers of the most modern types.

All other surface warships (including river craft) are to be concentrated in German naval bases to be designated by the Allies and the United States of America, and are to be paid-off and completely disarmed and placed under the supervision of the

Allies and the United States of America. All vessels of the auxiliary fleet (trawlers, motor-vessels, etc.) are to be disarmed. All vessels specified for internment shall be ready to leave German ports seven days after the signing of the armistice. Directions of the voyage will be given by wireless. Note – A declaration has been signed by the Allied delegates and handed to the German delegates to the effect that in the event of ships not being handed over owing to the mutinous state of the Fleet, the Allies reserve the right to occupy Heligoland as an advanced base to enable them to enforce the terms of the armistice. The German delegates have, on their part, signed a declaration that they will recommend the Chancellor to accept this.

XXIV. The Allies and the United States of America shall have the right to sweep up all minefields and obstructions laid by Germany outside German territorial waters, and the positions of these are to be indicated.

XXV. Freedom of access to and from the Baltic to be given to the naval and mercantile marines of the Allied and Associated Powers. To secure this the Allies and the United States of America shall be empowered to occupy all German forts, fortifications, batteries, and defence works of all kinds in all the entrances from the Kattegat into the Baltic, and to sweep up all mines and obstructions within and without German territorial waters without any questions of neutrality being raised and the positions of all such mines and obstructions are to be indicated.

XXVI. The existing blockade conditions set up by the Allied and Associated Powers are to remain unchanged, and all German merchant ships found at sea are to remain liable to capture. The Allies and United States contemplate the provisioning of Germany during the armistice as shall be found necessary.

XXVII. All naval aircraft are to be concentrated and immobilised in German bases to be specified by the Allies and the United States of America.

XXVIII. In evacuating the Belgian coasts and ports Germany shall abandon all merchant ships, tugs, lighters, cranes, and all other harbour materials, all materials for inland navigation, all aircraft and air materials and stores, all arms and armaments, and all stores and apparatus of all kinds.

XXIX. All Black Sea ports are to be evacuated by Germany; all Russian warships of all descriptions seized by Germany in the Black Sea are to be handed over to the Allies and the United States of America; all neutral merchant ships seized are to be released; all warlike and other materials of all kinds seized in those ports are to be returned, and German materials as specified in Clause XXVIII. are to be abandoned.

XXX. All merchant ships in German hands belonging to the Allied and Associated Powers are to be restored in ports to be specified by the Allies and the United States of America without reciprocity.

XXXI. No destruction of ships or of material to be permitted before evacuation, surrender, or restoration.

XXXII. The German Government shall formally notify the neutral Governments of the world – and particularly the Governments of Norway, Sweden, Denmark, and Holland – that all restrictions placed on the trading of their vessels with the Allied and Associated Countries, whether by the German Government or by private German interests, and, whether in return for specific concessions, such as the export of shipbuilding materials or not, are immediately cancelled.

XXXIII. No transfers of German merchant shipping of any description to any neutral flag are to take place after signature of the armistice.

DECLARATION OF ARMISTICE

XXXIV. The duration of the armistice is to be thirty-six days, with option to extend. During this period, on failure of execution of any of the above clauses, the armistice may be denounced by one of the contracting parties on forty-eight hours previous notice.

TIME-LIMIT FOR REPLY

XXXV. This armistice to be accepted or refused by Germany within seventy-two hours of notification.

Picture Credits

Page 82 – *Dance of Death*, Claggett Wilson. (*Smithsonian American Art Museum/Gift of Alice H. Rossin/Scala Archives*)

Page 83 – *Saviours of France*, Claggett Wilson. (*Smithsonian American Art Museum/Gift of Alice H. Rossin/Scala Archives*)

Page 84 – *The End of the War*, Horace Pippin. (*Philadelphia Museum of Art, Pennsylvania, PA, USA /Gift of Robert Carlen/ Bridgeman Images*)

Pages 86–7 – *Canadian War Memorial cartoon*, Augustus John. (*CWM 20110067-001/Beaverbrook Collection of War Art/ Canadian War Museum*)

Page 90 – *The Signing of Peace in the Hall of Mirrors, Versailles*, Sir William Orpen. (© *IWM, London, UK/Bridgeman Images*)

Page 91 – *Signing Peace in Versailles*, Sir William Orpen. (© *IWM, London, UK/Bridgeman Images*)

Page 94 – *Jan Smuts*, Sir William Orpen. (*Courtesy of the Parliament of the Republic of South Africa*)

Page 96 – *Lawrence of Arabia*, Augustus John. (*The Sullivan Collection/Bridgeman Images*)

Page 97 – *Prince Feisal I*, Augustus John. (*Private Collection/Photo* © *Christie's Images/Bridgeman Images*)

Page 99 – *Australian Prime Minister Hughes*, Augustus John. (*Art Gallery of New South Wales, Sydney, Australia/Gift of the Governor of the Commonwealth Bank 1946/Bridgeman Images*)

Page 100 – *The Marchesa Casati*, Augustus John. (*National Museum Wales/Bridgeman Images*)

Page 101 – *Elizabeth Asquith*, Augustus John. (*Laing Art Gallery, Newcastle-upon-Tyne, UK/*© *Tyne & Wear Archives & Museums/Bridgeman Images*)

Page 103 – *Woodrow Wilson*, Sir William Orpen. (*White House, Washington D.C., USA/Bridgeman Images*)

Page 105 – *Robert Cecil*, Sir William Orpen. (© *National Portrait Gallery, London*)

Page 108 – *Lloyd George at Versailles*, Sir William Orpen. (*Private Collection/Photo* © *Christie's Images/Bridgeman Images*)

Page 115 – *London Cenotaph*. (*Bridgeman Images*)

Page 117 – *The Cemetery, Étaples*, Sir John Lavery. (© *IWM Art.IWM ART 2884*)

Page 118 – Stone of Remembrance, designed by Sir Edwin Lutyens for the Commonwealth War Graves Commission. (© *Steve Daniels*)

Page 119 – *Étaples Military Cemetery, France*. (*Arterra/Philippe Clément/UIG/Bridgeman Images*)

Page 122 – *General Pershing*, Micheline Resco. (*Musee de l'Armee, Paris, France/Archives Charmet/Bridgeman Images*)

Pages 123–4 – *The Menin Gate Memorial*. (*Bridgeman Images*)

Page 127 – *Unknown British soldier*, Sir William Orpen. (© *IWM Art.IWM ART 4438*)

Page 130 – *Paths of Glory*, Christopher R.W. Nevinson. (*IWM/Bridgeman Images*)

Page 131 – *Harvest of Battle*, Christopher R.W. Nevinson. (© *IWM Art.IWM ART 1921*)

Page 132 – *Oppy Wood*, John Nash. (*IWM/Bridgeman Images*)

Page 133 – *A Two Year Old Steel Works*, Charles Holmes. (© *IWM Art.IWM ART 1216*)

Page 134 – *An Advanced Dressing Station*, Henry Tonks. (© *IWM Art.IWM ART 1922*)

Page 135 – *Divers at work repairing a torpedoed ship*, John Wheatley. (© *IWM Art.IWM ART 2245*)

Page 138 – *Siege of Kut-el-Amara seen from the air*, Richard Carline. (© *IWM Art.IWM ART 6349*)

Page 139 – *The Gorge at Wadi Fara*, Sydney Carline. (© *IWM Art.IWM ART 3138*)

Page 142 – *The Menin Road*, Paul Nash. (*IWM/Bridgeman Images*)

Page 143 – *The Moat at Kimble*, John Nash. (© *Tate, London 2018*)

Page 146 – *Self Portrait with severed hand*, Ludwig Kirchner. (*Allen Memorial Art Museum, Oberlin College, Ohio, USA/Charles F. Olney Fund/Bridgeman Images*)

Page 147 – *Skull*, Otto Dix. (*Minneapolis Institute of Arts, MN, USA/The John R. Van Derlip Fund and gift of funds from Alfred and Ingrid Lenz Harrison and the Regis Foundation/Bridgeman Images* © *The Estate of Otto Dix/ DACS*)

Page 148 – *Soldiers Begging (Monument to Unknown Prostheses)*, Heinrich Hoerle. (*Von der Heydt-Museum Wuppertal/Photo: Antje Zeis-Loi, Medienzentrum Wuppertal*)

Page 149 – *War cripples*, Otto Dix. (© *SZ Photo/Scherl/Bridgeman Images/*© *The Estate of Otto Dix/DACS*)

Page 151 – *Stormtroopers advancing*, Otto Dix. (*Minneapolis Institute of Arts, MN, USA/The John R. Van Derlip Fund and gift of funds from Alfred and Ingrid Lenz Harrison and the Regis Foundation/Bridgeman Images* © *The Estate of Otto Dix/DACS*)

Page 152 – *Pillars of Society*, George Grosz. (*Nationalgalerie, Berlin, Germany/Bridgeman Images/*© *The Estate of George Grosz/ DACS*)

Page 154 – *Gustav Stresemann*, Augustus John. (*Albright-Knox Art Gallery, Buffalo, New York/*© *Estate of Augustus John/ Bridgeman Images*)

Page 155 – *Beat the Whites with the Red Wedge*, El Lissitzky. (*Private Collection/Photo* © *Christie's Images/Bridgeman Images*)

Page 156 – *Several circles*, Wassily Kandinsky.